Myth Busters:

Why Health Reform Always Goes Awry

Greg Scandlen

Greg Scandlen

TABLE OF CONTENTS

Introduction

I came in to healthcare as a novice and a skeptic. I had been working as a community organizer among the poor neighborhoods of Portland, Maine, and then as the director of the Maine Public Interest Research Group (PIRG), a Ralph Nader inspired consumer advocacy organization.

In the first job, I saw first hand how the policy elite was willing to inflict remedies on other people they would never tolerate in their own lives. We had a welfare system that forbade any male involvement with needy families. Case workers would actually invade a mother's home looking for any sign of adult male presence, like clothes in the closets or male items in the bathroom. And then they wondered about the breakdown of families.

We had a few public housing projects that crammed together the poorest, least functional families in poorly constructed buildings as far out of sight as possible. And then the bureaucrats marveled that the residents were depressed and hopeless.

We had an urban renewal program that destroyed blocks of viable low income housing because of "blight," which was partly defined as "mixed use" – having residential, commercial, and light industrial properties integrated in the same neighborhood. Never mind that the commercial and industrial businesses provided jobs within walking distance for people without a lot of skills and no transportation. Some of the areas that were spared from destruction would go on to be rehabbed and turned into charming and vital tourist attractions.

PIRG worked on very mild consumer projects, like the monopoly funeral homes had on the sale of caskets and the need for a "lemon law" – the ability of buyers to return defective cars to dealers without penalty.

None of this work paid very well and I had three children, so when Blue Cross advertised that it needed someone to re-write its contracts into "plain English" I borrowed a suit and applied for the job. I was 31 years old.

That was my introduction into the world of health policy. Working with the legal department to understand every line of our consumer contract was a way to learn the business very quickly, I soon moved into the research department where I developed a new hospice benefit and worked on legislative issues.

Here I discovered that most of the upper management in this (and other) health insurance companies were well-meaning, non-confrontational people who thought they were providing a valuable service. They were like deer in the headlights when faced with hostile advocates for one cause or another. I used to accompany them to legislative hearings that demanded they cover substance abuse treatment, or nurse midwives, or chiropractors, or any of a hundred other special interest items. The response was always, "Well, we could, but it would cost a lot and we haven't seen any demand for it in the market." This response, while true, did little to deter passionate advocates who wanted a piece of the health insurance pie. No one of these proposals would really cost all that much, but when taken together they became a major cause of the rise in health insurance costs (see Chapter 11 on "Mandated Benefits").

Equally interesting to me was the emotional attitude of both sides in these disputes. The insurance executives were fearful. They would walk into the hearing room all clustered together wearing good suits, sit together, and never talk to other people in the room. I would sit apart from them and strike up conversations with the advocates. I learned a lot from doing that, including that the advocates weren't all that serious about their passion. It was a pose they put on for the legislators. It would have been pretty easy to diffuse with better communications.

Myth Busters

After five years of this the national Blue Cross Blue Shield Association recruited me to come to Washington, DC to work in their state affairs office. There, too, I learned a lot, including that people who work for national trade associations in Washington often don't know what they are talking about. They are almost always former Hill staffers who have never worked a day for the industries they represent. They may know something about Congress, but even there their knowledge is limited. Often they got an internship right out of college and have never worked in a political campaign, so they don't really understand the ocean their bosses swim in. In fact, association staffers usually have more loyalty to their friends on the Hill than to the industries they represent. There are exceptions, of course, but the principle holds.

Even more surprising to me was the realization that the people in DC are not "the best and the brightest" I was expecting. Rather they are often pretty mediocre talents who become powerful simply because they work in Washington rather than in Tallahassee, Florida or Frankfurt, Kentucky.

So, as I became more enmeshed in Health Policy circles, I started applying the same skeptical eye to what they were advocating. It turned out that almost every initiative was doomed to failure, simply because the advocates failed to look at all the evidence and rarely questioned their own assumptions. Instead they embraced some idea that could fit on a bumper sticker, sought out support for the idea, and ignored anything that was contrary.

Anyone who questioned the assumptions was seen as getting in the way of well-intentioned progress -- mocked, shunned and reviled. This enforced a kind of "group think" that disregarded contrary evidence and led to some horrific public policies. As a result, nearly every reform that has been embraced over the past fifty years has failed. Actually, not just failed, but made conditions worse than they were before the reforms were adopted.

The people who actually deliver health care services, the hospitals, nurses, and especially the doctors, have been whip-sawed back and forth trying to comply with new laws and regulations, and then undoing the compliance when the policy is repealed or amended.

With every new iteration of policy the providers of services have to run out and hire attorneys, accountants, software programmers, and compliance officers just to avoid running afoul of the new rules. Of course this all costs a great deal of money and contributes absolutely nothing to patient care.

What follows are thirty examples of specific initiatives that have contributed to the mess we have created. Most of these have been previously published either in the Health Policy Blog of the National Center for Policy Analysis or in The Federalist. I stop just before the enactment of the Affordable Care Act (Obamacare), because Obamacare didn't break new ground. Rather, it is a compilation and doubling down on all the mistakes that took place in the previous decades.

Myth Busters #1: Roemer's Law

If you ask anyone who has studied health economics or health policy in the last fifty years, "what is Roemer's Law?" they will each be able to tell you in an instant — "that means a built bed is a filled bed."

Milton Roemer, MD, was a researcher and professor, mostly at UCLA, who spent a lifetime (he died in 2001) advocating for national health systems around the world. He was involved in creating the World Health Organization in 1951 and Saskatchewan's provincial single payer system in 1953.[1] His "law" was based on a single study he did in 1959 [2] that found a correlation between the number of hospital beds per person and the rate of hospital days used per person. That's it. That is the whole basis for "Roemer's Law."

"A built bed is a filled bed." This little bumper sticker slogan has been the foundation of American health policy for 60 years. Hundreds of laws, massive programs, thousands of regulations at the federal, state and local levels of government, all have been based on this slogan. It is the source of such concepts as "provider induced demand," and has resulted in centralized health planning, Certificate of Need regulations, managed care, and everything else currently on the table. Yet this "law" is both verifiably untrue and illogical.

There is a kernel of truth to it. When third-party payers pick up the tab, the usual tension between buyer and seller doesn't exist. The buyer has no reason to resist excessive prices if someone else pays the bill.

---

[1] A brief biography of Milton Roemer may be found here:
http://newsroom.ucla.edu/releases/Milton-I-Roemer-Pioneering-UCLA-2053
[2] https://www.ncbi.nlm.nih.gov/pubmed/13644010

But the believers in Roemer's Law take that core idea to Alice-In-Wonderland proportions. They argue that, therefore, whenever a health care provider wants to make more money, it simply has to sell more — more capacity equals more sales without end. So, the only way to reduce this endless consumption is to limit the capacity — place strict controls on the availability of services.

But the notion fails for several reasons:

- People are not eager to enter the hospital, even when the cost is zero. Hospitals are miserable places to spend time. Folks are not lined up around the corner just waiting for an opportunity to be admitted to the hospital if only there were more beds available.
- If the "law" were true, hospital occupancy should approach 100 percent at all times. In fact, occupancy rates vary considerably over time and from place to place. Some years they are up, other years they are down. For example from 1970 to 2000 national hospital occupancy rates dropped from 77 percent to 67 percent, according to the **National Center for Health Statistics.** [3] Apparently one-third of "built beds" were *not* "filled beds" during this period. In 2005 occupancy rates varied from 92 percent in Delaware to 53 percent in Idaho.

So, Roemer's Law is statistically untrue, it is behaviorally untrue, yet it has been the basis for virtually all of the health policy initiatives of the last 60 years, including Certificate of Need, national health planning, hospital rate-setting, Health Maintenance Organizations, and more recently, Accountable Care Organizations, pay-for-performance, and comparative effectiveness research.

---

[3] Hospitals, beds, and occupancy rates, by type of ownership and size of hospital: https://www.cdc.gov/nchs/data/hus/hus07.pdf#page=368

Myth Busters

No wonder all these efforts were doomed to fail — they were all based on a false premise, as we will look at in future chapters.

Greg Scandlen

Myth Busters #2: Hysterectomies in Lewiston, Maine

One of the consequences of **Roemer's Law** has been the idea of "provider induced demand," and the general notion that everything that happens in health care is because some greedy doctor has deemed it. This means that patients don't count. What patients may want is irrelevant.

Nowhere is this better illustrated than in Jack Wennberg's early work on "small area variation" in medical practice.

I was working in the research department at Blue Cross Blue Shield of Maine from 1979 to 1984 and we offered the use of our claims files for his research. He had already done some work in Vermont looking at variations in the rate of tonsillectomies in various towns. He found that in some places physicians surgically remove tonsils at a much greater rate than they do in other places. He concluded that this was an example of Roemer's Law in effect — scalpel-happy physicians were too quick to order up surgery in some places, but not in others.

The most startling variation he found in Maine — and the one that put him on the map — was the difference between the rate of hysterectomies in Lewiston and Wiscasset, just 35 miles apart. The chance of a woman getting a hysterectomy in Lewiston by the time she was 70-years old was 70%. In Wiscasset it was a fraction of that.

Wennberg, in keeping with the narrative he developed in Vermont, decided that this was because physicians in Lewiston were eager to cut while their fellows in Wiscasset were not. Curious. Why should that be? He didn't know but speculated that maybe they were trained at different medical schools, or somehow the profession in one town had grown to be more aggressive than those 35 miles away.

Hmm, is Maine so very isolated that doctors in Lewiston never talk to their colleagues just 35 miles away? That was certainly not my experience. In fact, Maine was not exactly crawling with physicians, so opportunities for professional bonding would necessarily include physicians from many different towns. In fact, in a search of a **physician directory compiled by the Maine Medical Center,** [4] I could find only 45 Obstetricians/Gynecologists in the entire state. Is it really credible that those only 35 miles apart would not be talking with each other?

Completely missed in Wennberg's analysis was the possibility that maybe it wasn't the physicians who dictated what happened, but the patients. There are stark differences in the populations of the two towns. Wiscasset was an old fishing village with a largely Yankee (Protestant) population. Lewiston was an industrial mill town with a predominantly French-Canadian (Roman Catholic) population. It is far more likely that women in Lewiston were using hysterectomies as a form of birth control that was acceptable to the Church, especially in the early 1970s before birth control pills were widely available. Many of us who lived in Maine at the time, thought this was pretty obvious, and were surprised and amused at the attention Wennberg's study got.

Even more surprising is that Wennberg's study was still getting attention thirty years later. In 2009, National Public Radio (NPR) published a major article, **"The Telltale Wombs of Lewiston, Maine."** [5] The piece by Alix Spiegel is gushing about Wennberg, calling him, "a certified guru — a man whose insights underlie many of the arguments you currently hear about health reform...." It adds, "Over the past 40 years, he has completely transformed our understanding of what's going on in the U.S. health care system."

---

[4] No longer available on-line.
[5] See: http://www.npr.org/templates/story/story.php?storyId=113571111

Myth Busters

The article goes on to say there were two possible explanations for differences in medical practice — "The first explanation was that doctor behavior was somehow to blame. The second explanation was that it was the patients; that people in some areas were just much sicker than people in other areas, or maybe just wanted more services for some reason." The article says Wennberg looked at the possibility of differences in patient demographics and level of sickness and dismissed it.

This is unconvincing because it doesn't say whether he gave any weight to issues like religious differences rather than just differences in disease severity. It is a profound weakness in research that treats patients like statistics rather than fully developed human beings. Statistics fail to capture the most important aspects of human beings, such as personal values or emotional condition. This is precisely why medicine has always (until now) been centered on a personal relationship between a doctor and a patient.

Wennberg insisted that, "it was doctors, not patients, who drove medical consumption, and all kinds of things influenced the decisions a doctor makes when a patient enters his office."

Actually, this reveals a bias among the educated elite that "common" working people are not bright enough or involved enough to have much effect on the world around them. An academic like Jack Wennberg assumes that all decisions must be coming from people like himself — other educated elitists. "The people" are just the raw material the elite uses in their machinations. So, to the extent "the people" have opinions, preferences, fears, hopes, values, or expectations, these are just characteristics that have to be managed by the people who know best.

After much discussion, the NPR article finally gets to the heart of the matter — money. It says, "the truth is the decisions made by your physician when you enter his office are profoundly influenced by the way that doctors get paid in this country." It quotes Gordon Smith, the non-physician head of the Maine Medical Association, as saying, "If you pay people more, the more things they do, they're going to do more things."

That is the conventional thinking among academics these days, and it goes back, once again, to Roemer's Law ("a built bed is a filled bed") and the idea of "provider induced demand." Once again, that notion is driving most of the thinking in health policy today.

But Wennberg's research, if anything, contradicts that very idea. It does *not* support it. Physicians in Wiscasset and Lewiston were all under the same payment system. They were all subject to the same incentives. If it were the payment system that drove their decision-making, they would all be practicing in the same way. The fact that they practice differently strongly suggests it is *not* the payment system that drives behavior.

But once again public policy is driven by an idea that could fit on a bumper sticker — "Greedy Doctors rip out wombs for fun and profit" — even though the doctors in two towns 35 miles apart behaved very differently.

Still, Wennberg went on to create the Dartmouth Health Atlas,[6] which lives on and continues to distort data and influence public policy (See Chapter 25 for more on Dartmouth's research), all based on this original idea that the payment system incentivizes greedy doctors to over treat hapless patients — but only in some towns.

---

[6] http://www.dartmouthatlas.org/

Myth Busters #3: National Health Planning

One of the most serious consequences of **Roemer's Law** was the creation of national health planning.

The National Health Planning and Resources Development Act was enacted in 1974 to require states to establish elaborate bureaucracies to control the growth of hospitals and other health care facilities. These agencies included Health Systems Agencies (HSAs), State Health Planning and Development Agencies (SHPDAs), Statewide Health Coordinating Councils (SHCCs), and a host of other committees and agencies. These efforts were designed to implement Certificate of Need (CON) programs, through which hospitals and other facilities that wished to make capital outlays would have to get prior approval from the agencies.[7]

This law was enacted out of recognition that the massive infusion of federal funds into the existing health care system contributed to inflationary increases in the cost of health care. Indeed, the enactment of Medicare and Medicaid in 1965 resulted in a vast increase of federal spending in the health care system:

- In 1965, state and local governments spent $4.3 billion on health care, while the federal government spent only $2.9 billion.
- Two years later, state and local spending rose 28 percent to $5.5 billion, but federal spending went up 234 percent to $9.7 billion.
- By 1970, state expenditures would rise to $9.9 billion, and federal spending would reach $17.7 billion — over six times what had been spent five years earlier. [8]

---

[7] Terree P. Wasley, What Has Government Done to Our Health Care?, Cato Institute, Washington, DC, 1992, p. 71-72.

This, naturally, resulted in enormous health care inflation. The rate of annual increase in health care spending was very close to the increase in Gross Domestic Product in 1965 and 1966, but immediately it began to rise at double the rate.

Rate of Increase in Gross Domestic Product and National Health Expenditures as a percentage from previous year, 1965 – 1970

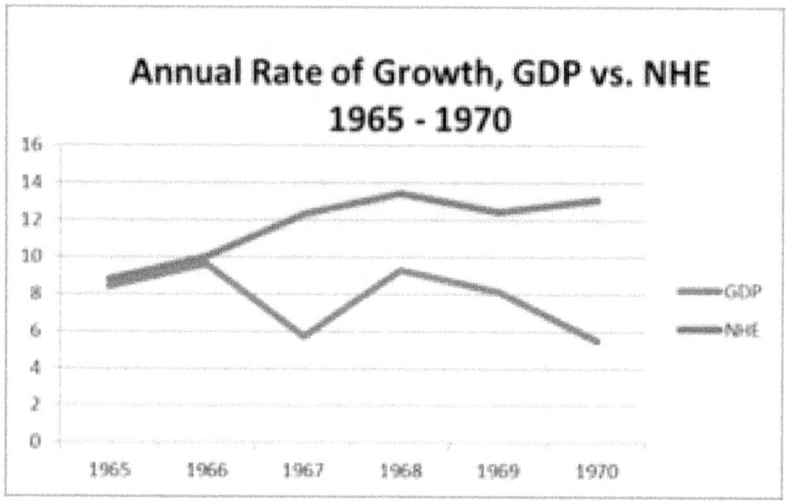

Source: Katherine R. Levit, et.al., "National Health Expenditures, 1990," Health Care Financing Review, Fall, 1991.

The panic among the health policy community was stark. The then-HCFA administrator, Stuart Altman, who oversaw the Medicare and Medicaid programs, was interviewed in 2001, as saying:

> "When I was 32 years old, I became the chief regulator in this country for health care. At that point, we were spending about 7.5 percent of our GDP on health care. The prevailing wisdom was that we were spending too much,

---

[8] Katherine R. Levit, et.al., "National Health Expenditures, 1990," Health Care Financing Review, Fall, 1991.

and that if we hit 8 percent, our system would collapse." [9]

Two other scholars were equally agitated. Kenneth Friedman and Stuart Rakoff wrote:

> "The thrust towards greater government regulation of health services arises primarily from a single source; astronomical increases in cost. Total expenditures for health services have more than tripled since 1965, exceeding $118 billion in FY 1975. The proportion of GNP devoted to health care has grown from 5.9 to 8.3 percent." [10]

So, we have a massive infusion of new money into the health care system, which raised demand for services, which resulted in an astonishing increase in prices. And how do the dunces in health policy respond? They enacted a massive and mandatory health planning system, which was intended to *reduce* the supply of services — precisely the *wrong* reaction at a time of high inflation due to rising demand.

But Roemer's Law says that demand is irrelevant. The only thing that counts is supply. Inflation in health care is caused solely by providers "inducing" demand to enrich themselves. Reduce the number of suppliers, and you reduce the costs of health care.

Not surprisingly, this approach did not work and health inflation continued unabated. In fact, the year before Health Planning was adopted, the Gross Domestic Product grew faster than health spending (in 1973, the GDP rose 11.7% while NHE rose 10.9%). After it was adopted in 1974, health spending was back on a rampage with the exception of one year.

The main law was repealed in 1982, but billions of dollars and

---

[9] Stuart Altman, interviewed by Andrew Osterland in CFO Magazine, June, 2001, p.75.
[10] Kenneth Friedman & Stuart H. Rakoff, Toward a National Health Policy, Lexington Books, Lexington, MA, 1977, p. 108

years of effort were wasted on an idea that never made any sense in the first place. And no one was ever held to account.

Myth Busters #4: Hospital Rate Setting

With the repeal of the Health Planning Act in 1982, a lot of health policy wonks found themselves out of work. They had to come up with something new to earn a living and justify their PhDs.

They had learned a very expensive lesson — that reducing supply at a time of growing demand is a bad idea because it results in rising prices. This is something most people learn less expensively in Econ101, but it seems to have escaped the health policy community, which often reflects Ivy Baker Priest's famous quote, "I am often wrong, but never in doubt."

So, they decided that this time they would control prices. I was still In Maine, when we adopted a hospital rate setting system in 1983. This initiative was based largely on a study published in the *New England Journal of Medicine* in 1980, "Hospital Cost Inflation under State Rate Setting Programs," by Brian Biles, Carl Schramm, and Graham Atkinson. [11] The article concluded,

> "... the average annual rate of increase in hospital costs in (the six) rate-setting states has been 11.2 per cent, as compared with an average annual rate of increase of 14.3 per cent in states without such programs."

In 1986 the authors updated that information through 1984 in an article in *Health Affairs*, "Controlling Hospital Cost Inflation: New Perspectives on State Rate Setting." [12]

It is interesting that these were state-based systems. With Ronald Reagan as president it was unlikely that private sector price controls could have become federal law. But the health policy

---

[11] http://www.nejm.org/doi/full/10.1056/NEJM198009183031203
[12] http://content.healthaffairs.org/content/5/3/22.full.pdf+html?sid=da3e048d-fc2a-44dd-aee5-0a8dfb7f761e

community is nothing if not inventive – when blocked at the federal level, it will switch to the states to accomplish its goals.

Of course, the six rate-setting states (Connecticut, Maryland, Massachusetts, New Jersey, New York, and Washington) cited in the original article started out as probably the most expensive and wasteful states in the nation. That is why they were prompted to adopt these systems in the first place. There was already plenty of fat to be trimmed, which would not be true for other states.

Indeed, the Health Affairs article reported that the non-regulated states had a per capita hospital cost of $107.02 in 1972, while the six states that adopted the price controls were spending $135.08 per person. Further, these costs were spread over a much larger hospitalized population in the non-regulated states, which had an admissions rate of 152.8 per thousand in 1972, compared to 131.1 per thousand in the states that adopted regulations.

Usually in research if there is a self-selected sample being studied, the researchers look to see what might distinguish the sample from the rest of the population and adjust their findings accordingly. Not so for health policy advocates who are so eager to push their preferred remedies that they ignore what should be standard techniques of research.

The original study mentioned above completely overlooked many pertinent differences between the six regulated states and the forty-five (including DC) non-regulated areas. Obvious differences include that the six states tended to be no-growth or low-growth states, so they had little need for new hospital construction. They also tend to be high Medicaid enrollment states, but also with higher average incomes than the non-regulated states. Other possible differences that would have been worth exploring include the relative percentage of uninsured, the ratio of teaching hospitals, the availability of non-hospital alternatives such as home health services or free standing surgical services, and the presence of for-profit hospitals. All of these differences could have had a profound effect on the viability of hospital rate setting in the various states but none were even considered.

As it was, what the research discovered was that after 13 years of experience:

- The high-cost states remained high cost.
- These states began with lower rates of admissions, and ended with lower rates of admissions.
- They began with lower operating margins and ended with lower operating margins.

Yet somehow the researchers concluded that hospitals in the regulated states were "more efficient" than those in the non-regulated states, though it would seem that having fewer admissions at higher costs while maintaining low profit margins would be a slam dunk argument that these regulated hospitals were anything but more efficient.

Such one-sided research was persuasive enough to the "health policy community" that 30 states ended up adopting similar rate setting programs during the 1980s. Here is yet another example of an unscrutinized idea that led to yet another failure — but only after more wasted money and time.

In 1997 Health Affairs published another article with a somewhat different tone. This was **"Tracking the Demise of State Hospital Rate Setting,"** by John McDonough. [13] The article said, "Now, in the mid-1990s, state rate setting is nearly gone; most major systems have been deregulated during the last ten years." (Ultimately these systems were repealed by every state but Maryland.) The article explained that the growing managed care companies thought they could negotiate lower hospital rates than were available through price-controls, and that the regulators themselves agreed their rules were "incomprehensible."

---

[13] http://content.healthaffairs.org/content/16/1/142.full.pdf+html?sid=a70863ff-a349-4aa4-90ab-55a3bf32e1b4

Not mentioned by the author, but fairly obvious, was the reality that once state government becomes responsible for setting prices, it also becomes responsible for assuring the solvency of the facilities. Inefficient facilities are protected from failure, and any decision to close a hospital becomes a political, not an economic, one. A threatened facility can generate enough political support to keep its doors open, even when it makes no economic sense to do so.

In any case, once again an idea was tried and failed miserably at the cost of many billions of dollars and who knows how many lives lost or destroyed. All on an idea that was poorly thought through in the first place.

Myth Busters #5: Certificate of Need

So, national health planning was **repealed,** and hospital rate setting was **repealed in all but Maryland** — all after wasting many billions of dollars and who knows how much pain and suffering to patients.

Yet one similar command and control program keeps ticking along — Certificate of Need (CON). Certificate of Need programs require hospitals and many other facilities to get permission from a state agency before making capital investments in new buildings, equipment, or services. The thinking behind it is, once again, **based on Roemer's Law**_— the more providers there are, the more spending there will be, because patients are gullible puppets doing whatever the Greedy Doctors tell them to do.

The National Conference of State Legislatures (NCSL) **publishes state-by-state information on state CON laws,** [14] including the scope of affected entities and contact information for each program. It also includes a brief history of the program.

As the NCSL points out, one of the earliest and most vigorous advocates of CON was the American Hospital Association (AHA). If this surprises you, you might want to consider getting out of the office more often.

You may think we live in a capitalist economy, or in some cases socialist. But in health care, we are still in a mercantilist system, featuring a guild of select providers, who are protected from competition by the government.

The support of the AHA once again belies Roemer's Law. If it were true that "a built bed is a filled bed," the AHA would oppose CON because demand is unlimited and there are plenty of patients to fill every bed that could ever be built, and plenty of money to

---

[14] NCSL, "CON, Certificate of Need State Laws," August 25, 2016.
http://www.ncsl.org/research/health/con-certificate-of-need-state-laws.aspx

pay for it. In fact, the AHA knows perfectly well that demand is limited, and it wants its members to be the only ones allowed to fill that limited demand.

These incumbent providers will fight tooth and nail to prevent competitors from coming in to their market area. As a result, prospective competitors have to spend very large amounts of money and time on attorneys, economists, accountants, architects, and public relations firms just on the approval process.

Even then, they may not be able to overcome the corruption of the approval boards, which opens the door for more corruption. After all, when a mere handful of people on a panel determine whether your $300 million hospital will be built or not, it is hard not to slip them some favors to get the okay. Illinois was the poster child of such graft under the reign of Gov. Rob Blagojevich. [15]

Political corruption aside, CON is a fundamentally flawed idea. It assumes that each community has only so many consumers who can sensibly fill only so many beds, so any "overbuilding" is wasteful. (One might think that it would be wasteful only of the investors' dollars — if they are overbuilding, they will lose their money. But that is not how social planners think.)

In fact, a new facility is not confined to serving the number of patients located in that community. A world-class facility will attract patients from all over the country, and from all over the globe.

For example, Washington state blocked the construction of new facilities that might have prospered by serving citizens from British Columbia and the Pacific Rim, because the CON Board tallied up the number of Seattle residents, divided by the number of

---

[15] See, for example Mark L. Wang, Crain's Chicago Business, "State decisions on Mercy, Centegra renew questions on certificates of need" September 13, 2012.
http://www.chicagobusiness.com/article/20120913/NEWS03/120919878/state-decisions-on-mercy-centegra-renew-questions-on-certificates-of-need

existing beds, and declared there were already enough beds to serve Seattle. Thus, the state killed off what was a promising economic development program for Seattle, one that might have created thousands of new jobs and millions in new tax revenue. For more about Washington state's CON program, see **"The Failure of Government Central Planning: Washington's Medical Certificate of Need Program,"** by John Barnes. [16]

CON also stifles innovation and improved quality. Existing providers who are accustomed to doing things in a certain way are protected from being challenged by new, more efficient, competitors. In 2004, the Federal Trade Commission and the Department of Justice released a joint study, **"Improving Health Care: A Dose of Competition,"** [17] urging states to:

> "Reconsider whether Certificate of Need Programs best serve their citizens' health care needs. On balance, the DOJ and the FTC believe that such programs are not successful in containing health care costs, and they pose serious anticompetitive risks that usually outweigh their purported economic benefits."

At a minimum these "purported benefits" should include some reduction in the costs of health care spending. But Christopher Conover and Frank Sloan of Duke University were unable to detect such an effect in a study they conducted, **"Does Removing Certificate-of-Need Regulations Lead to a Surge in Health Care Spending?"** [18] The authors write:

> "Mature CON programs are associated with a modest (5 percent) long-term reduction in acute care spending per capita, but not with a significant reduction in total per capita spending. There is no evidence of a surge in

[16] http://www.washingtonpolicy.org/publications/detail/new-study-highlights-the-failure-of-washingtons-medical-certificate-of-need-program
[17] https://www.ftc.gov/reports/improving-health-care-dose-competition-report-federal-trade-commission-department-justice
[18] http://jhppl.dukejournals.org/content/23/3/455.abstract

acquisition of facilities or in costs following removal of CON regulations. Mature CON programs also result in a slight (2 percent) reduction in bed supply but higher costs per day and per admission, along with higher hospital profits. CON regulations generally have no detectable effect on diffusion of various hospital-based technologies."

That study was conducted in 1998. Today it is far more likely that CON will be shown to have raised costs after the dramatic consolidation of the hospital industry, especially in CON states. Monopoly providers can charge whatever they like, and have no fear that health plans will refuse to include them in their networks. How many people will enroll in a health plan that doesn't cover the only hospital in their locale?

CON has been an amazing success story for the American Hospital Association and its members, but it has been disastrous for the American consumer and taxpayer.

Myth Busters #6: Business Coalitions on Health

This series of failures so far has focused on the big government initiatives that have failed over the past forty years, but there have also been a whole lot of smaller efforts that have been equally futile.

One example is from an article written by Health Affairs editor John Iglehart and M.D. Egdahl in 1983, "**Health Cost Management at the Community Level: Doctors, Hospitals and Industry.**" [19] It is based on a "conference on health cost management held at Boston University's Health Policy Institute."

Like many such articles this one is full of promises by well-meaning people who have convinced themselves and others that with the right incentives and the right management skills everything can be put right in health care. It is the original "Hope and Change" campaign. There could hardly have been a more stellar cast of participants. I will list them at the end of this chapter to emphasize the point.

The premise of the conference was based on a whole new idea — health care coalitions made up of representatives of business, labor, hospital administrators, and health plans. These coalitions (it was thought) would create a new era of efficient management and accountability at the community level. The article notes that:

> "The Robert Wood Johnson Foundation created a new program that invested some $16 million in community-based projects that seek to implement innovations intended to moderate the cost of medical care. The Pew Memorial Trust of Philadelphia and the John A. Hartford Foundation

---

[19] http://content.healthaffairs.org/content/2/3/115.full.pdf+html?sid=60937966-f4e3-48a2-8c2d-ba6181c2421a

of New York City also invested significant amounts of their philanthropic funds in locally sponsored projects that seek to improve the existing delivery system through private means rather than government action."

The conference looked especially at efforts in Rochester, New York (global budgets for hospitals), and New Jersey (an early DRG payment system), but also at smaller programs in Tennessee, Delaware, and Alabama.

I won't go into detailed descriptions of the programs other than to say all were based on the Roemer's Law idea that greedy doctors needlessly hospitalize innocent patients, either to enrich themselves or because they are lazy. It was thought that effective management of physicians by bureaucrats and business executives would curtail these practices. The article quotes, for instance, Don Bradley, president of the Morristown (NJ) hospital as saying that the state's DRG program is more than just a payment system:

> "It is a medical management system, too. . . . At long last now, I have got something to talk to a physician about in terms of his rate of consumption for a similar procedure compared to one of the members of his peer group."

Right, but of course the time Mr. Bradley (and dozens of others) spend lecturing physicians is time spent away from actually caring for patients.

Already, when this article was written, there were questions about how effective any of this would be. The authors write:

> "Although there is little evidence to date that local physicians have markedly altered the ways they practice, the fact that the hospital in which they work can keep savings from efficiency provides the basis for ongoing dialogue between hospital management and the medical staff."

The authors add:

Myth Busters

"The complexity of the nation's health system is such that, even if a widespread decrease in average length-of-stay were to be achieved, there is no guarantee of savings without some shrinkage of the hospital system."

And illustrating how Roemer's Law has poisoned the discussion:

"...if patients who would not have been hospitalized fill the empty beds freed up as a result of greater physician efficiency, overall health costs may increase...."

Once again, there is an assumption that there are endless ranks of patients lined up just eager to enter the first hospital with an empty bed as soon as a greedy doctor gives them permission.

Nearly 30 years later, after tens of millions of dollars from foundations and the active participation of top executives of Fortune 100 companies what is there to show for all this effort? As the chart below suggests, the addition of all these administrators has cost the health care system far more than it saved, and decreased efficiency as more time was spent on bureaucracy and less on patient care. All because the underlying premise was wrong — greedy doctors are *not* needlessly filling hospital beds to enrich themselves.

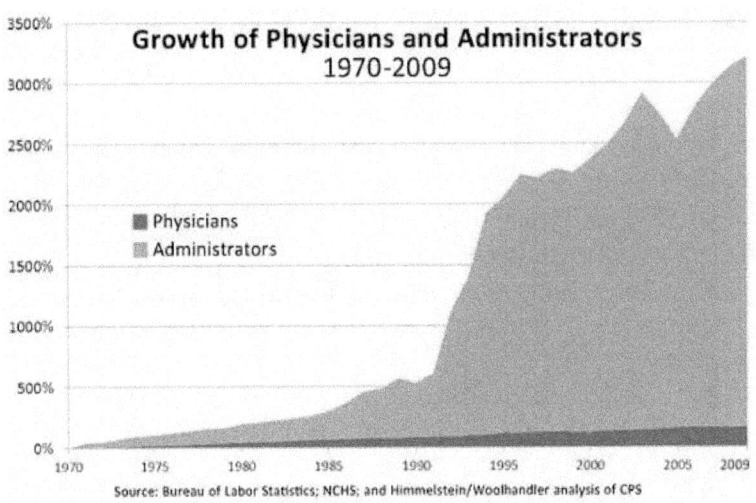

Growth of Physicians and Administrators 1970-2009

Source: Bureau of Labor Statistics; NCHS; and Himmelstein/Woolhandler analysis of CPS

Greg Scandlen

Monday Morning Quarterbacking is easy. In any enterprise we can look back on what has happened and talk about how it could have happened better. Obviously not every hospitalization will turn out to be appropriate, but we don't always know that ahead of time.

And some doctors are jerks. So are some Fortune 100 executives, hospital administrators, and health care economists. So what? I would wager that as a group physicians are more ethical and more caring than most other professions. If they over treat their patients, it is out of an abundance of caution rather than greed. When you have someone's life in your hands, you want to do everything possible to save them. This is a good thing.

Given the record of massive, epic failure from the "health policy community," I would much prefer to put my fate in the hands of any physician randomly found in the phone book than any of these bureaucrats.

Here is the promised list of conference participants:

- Robert Ambrose, M.D., Medical Director, Morristown Memorial Hospital, Morristown, New Jersey;
- John L. Bauer, Jr., Supervisor, Insurance Benefits, Armco Corporation, Middletown, Ohio;
- Martin Bael, Director, Corporate Employee Benefits, Eastman Kodak Company, Rochester, New York;
- Robert N. Beck, Executive Vice-President, Bank of America, San Francisco, California;
- Don Bradley, President, Morristown Memorial Hospital, Morristown, New Jersey;
- Leo P. Brideau, Deputy Director, Patient Care Services, Strong Memorial Hospital, Rochester, New York;
- Anthony Cucuzzella, M.D., Chief, Physical Medicine and Rehabilitation Section, Wilmington Medical Center, Wilmington, Delaware;
- William Deans, Manager, Health Care Benefits Section, E.I. DuPont de Nemours Company, Wilmington, Delaware;

Myth Busters

- Patricia Drury, Assistant Director for Health Care Financing, John A. Hartford Foundation, New York, New York;
- Richard H. Egdahl, M.D., Director, Center for Industry and Health Care, Boston University, Boston, Massachusetts;
- Peter D. Fox, Ph.D., Principal, Lewin and Associates, Washington, D.C.;
- Harry S. Glass, Director, Programs in Health Utilization Management, Center for Industry and Health Care, Boston, Massachusetts;
- Willis B. Goldbeck, Director, Washington Business Group on Health, Washington, D.C.,
- Jerome H. Grossman, M.D., President, New England Medical Center, Boston, Massachusetts;
- C. Rollins Hanlon, M.D., Director, American College of Surgeons, Chicago, Illinois;
- James G. Harding, President, Wilmington Medical Center, Wilmington, Delaware;
- James A. Hathaway, M.D., Director, Medical Affairs, Allied Chemical Company, Morristown New Jersey;
- John Iglehart, Editor, Health Affairs, Project HOPE, Millwood, Virginia;
- Colin L. Kamperman, M.D., Medical Director, Aluminum Company of America, Alcoa, Tennessee;
- J. Joel May, Executive Director, New Jersey Hospital Research and Educational Trust, Princeton, New Jersey;
- Allston J. Morris, M. D., Vice-President, Medical Affairs, Wilmington Medical Center, Wilmington, Delaware;
- Peter W. Morris, M.D., Jefferson Country Medical Society, Birmingham, Alabama;
- Henry S. Nelson, M.D., Chilhowee Medical Park, Maryville, Tennessee;
- Warren Nestler, M.D., Vice- President, Quality Assurance, Overlook Hospital, Summit, New Jersey;
- Jan Peter Ozga, Associate Director for Health Care, U.S. Chamber of Commerce, Washington, D.C.;
- Arnold S. Relman, M.D., Editor, New England Journal of Medicine, Boston, Massachusetts;

Greg Scandlen

- James R. Robinson, Wilmington, Delaware;
- Floyd M. Smith, South Central Bell, Birmingham, Alabama;
- James S. Todd, M.D., Member, Board of Trustees, American Medical Association, Chicago, Illinois;
- Bruce C. Vladeck, Ph.D., Assistant Vice-President, Robert Wood Johnson Foundation, Princeton, New Jersey;
- Galen Wagner, M.D. Associate Professor of Cardiology, Director- Coronary Care, Duke University Medical Center, Durham, North Carolina;
- Stanley S. Wallack, Director, University Health Policy Consortium, Florence Heller Graduate School, Brandeis University, Waltham, Massachusetts;
- Diana Chapman Walsh, Director, Program Evaluation, Center for Industry and Health Care, Boston, Massachusetts;
- Richard Wardrop, General Manager, Compensation and Benefits, Aluminum Company of America, Pittsburgh, Pennsylvania;
- James Weadick, Associate Administrator, Blount Memorial Hospital, Maryville, Tennessee;
- Frank E. Young, M.D., Ph.D., Dean, University of Rochester School of Medicine and Dentistry, Rochester, New York.

Myth Busters #7: It's All the Doctors' Fault

Misguided public policy doesn't just come out of the blue. It percolates up from the swamp of academia, which develops the ideas and the terminology that end up crafting the laws and regulations Washington inflicts on the rest of us.

One example is **study from Health Affairs** that put the blame for America's health care problems squarely on them Greedy Doctors. A press release [20] announcing the study said:

> "Research appearing in the September issue of Health Affairs shows that physicians in the United States are paid more per service than doctors in other countries–in some cases double. There is also a far bigger gap between fees paid for primary care and fees paid for specialty care in the United States, compared to other countries. These higher fees in turn lead to higher incomes for US physicians than those earned by their foreign counterparts, and are the main driver of higher overall spending in the United States on physicians' services."

Well, not really. The article, "Higher Fees Paid to US Physicians Drive Higher Spending for Physician Services Compared to Other Countries," by Miriam Laugesen and Sherry Glied, is a pretty thin reed on which to hang such a sweeping conclusion.

In fact, the article shows how difficult it is (nearly impossible) to compare service payments between countries, something the authors acknowledge, though they prefer to call it "challenging."

As you're reading what follows, keep in mind the following chart from **Deloitte,** [21] which found that the majority of U.S. consumers

---

[20] http://www.healthaffairs.org/press/2011_09_08.php

feel they get their money's worth in out-of-pocket spending on physician services.

What We Value in Health Care

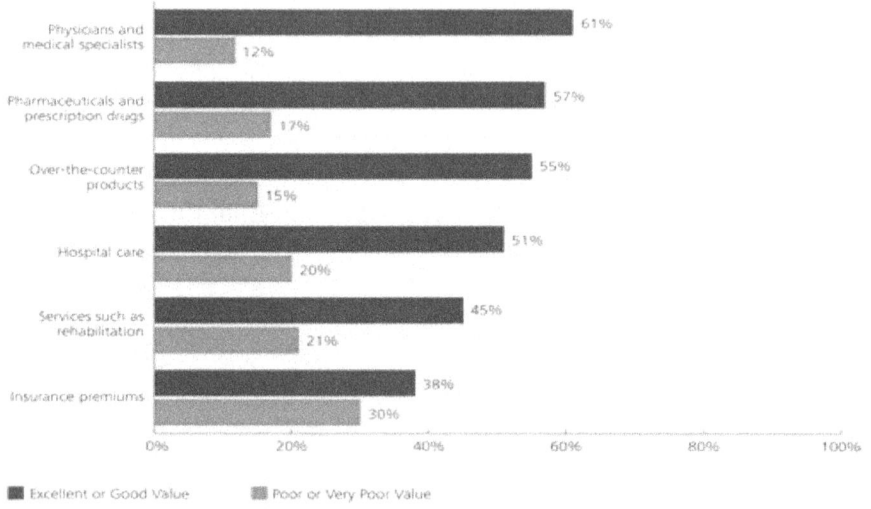

Note: Base for each percentage includes only respondents who spent money in the area.

Laugesen and Glied look at primary care and orthopedic surgery (hip replacements) in the U.S., U.K., Australia, Canada, France and Germany, but the payment system is different in each location, and the "service" may be defined differently as well. All of the countries involve a mixture of public and private payments and some have private payers supplementing the public payment. The authors go into great detail about these "challenges," but still not enough to make sense of it. For instance, surgeons in Germany are salaried, so how do they allocate the cost of a hip replacement against other services? They don't say. Many of these countries allow physicians to bill on top of the regular payment, but it isn't

---

[21] https://www.washingtonpost.com/blogs/ezra-klein/post/what-we-value-in-health-care-in-one-chart/2011/09/12/gIQAotAnMK_blog.html?utm_term=.fe03ed459278&wprss=ezra-klein

clear how much. In the U.S. private payer data on physician payment is proprietary, so the authors rely on HealthGrades reports, which may or may not be reliable.

But the authors satisfy themselves that they have squeezed out enough payment information to write about. Then, to get to "net physician income" they subtract "practice expenses" from the gross. But they don't have a word to say about what they mean by "practice expenses," how those expenses may vary between countries, or how they determined how much they cost. Presumably, the expenses will always include rent, utilities, staff salaries, and malpractice insurance costs, but what about physician time devoted to administration? Is that included or not? We don't have a hint.

The authors take some time to consider educational expenses, which in the U.S. is typically born by the physician, but not so much in other countries, but again this issue is more complicated than the authors are willing to admit. The closest they come is in noting that primary care physicians in the U.S. earn $27,000 more than those on the U.K., which is more than enough to offset the $21,300 annual cost of tuition for the American physician. Well, yes, I suppose it is — assuming everything else is equal, which is a big assumption.

Towards the end of the article, the authors also discuss (a little bit) the fact that higher physician payment in the U.S. may be due to the fact that all professionals in this country command higher wages than in those other countries. Medicine has to compete against business, engineering, law, and other high-earning professions to attract competent people. In one of their tables the authors report on per capita GDP and find the U.S. is much more prosperous than the other countries:

Per Capita GDP in Dollars, 2008

Austral.	Canada	France	Germ.	U.K.	U.S.
39,439	39,288	33,134	35,436	36,128	47,193

But they don't try to factor this into their conclusions at all. They might, for instance, have averaged the per capita GDP of the five other countries ($36,685) and found that the U.S. is higher by 28.6%, and used this "relative wealth factor" to adjust their results. But, no, that would not suit the pre-determined narrative of the Health Affairs editors.

Meanwhile, there are plenty of other questions that go unaddressed, including:

- Is the bundle of services the same in each country? What tests are performed during a visit with a primary care physician? Does the surgical fee for hip transplants include follow-up visits or rehabilitation?
- In some countries physicians pay for their own health insurance through taxes while in the U.S. they pay with after-tax income. Why not account for that difference in comparing incomes?
- Physicians in the U.S. make much use of Physician Assistants and other "physician extenders." Is the same true in other countries? If not, don't American physicians have more unpaid supervisory responsibility than in other countries?
- Similarly, an inordinate amount of physician time in the U.S. is spent on dealing with insurance company paperwork, prior approvals, appeals, and reviews. This time is subtracted from patient care and billable hours. Do other countries have similar issues?

Myth Busters

* Finally, a table included in the article shows a wide
variation in how health care expenses are allocated in each
country:

	Australia	Canada	France	Germany	U.K.	U.S.
Ambulatory	37.7%	28.9%	28.4%	30.8%	n/a	36.0%
(physician office)	(14.6)	(14.7)	(11.7)	(15.8)	n/a	(21.2)
Hospital	39.9%	28.9%	35.0%	29.4%	n/a	32.9%
Pharmaceuticals	14.3%	17.2%	16.4%	15.1%	11.8%	11.9%
Total reported	91.9%	75.0%	79.8%	75.3%	n/a	80.8%

This table raises all kinds of fascinating questions, such as where
does the rest of the money go? Presumably some of it goes to
nursing home or dental care, but is it credible that Australia has
virtually none of these services?

I don't know the answers to any of these questions, but these
researchers have done us all a disservice by not even asking them
or trying an answer them. Sadly, this is another example of
"research" that is selected to support a predetermined conclusion.

Is it any wonder that nothing we ever do in health policy actually
works?

Greg Scandlen

Myth Busters #8: Discovering Uncompensated Care

The fallacy of Roemer's Law ("a built bed is a filled bed") spawned an endless series of policy initiatives — national health planning, hospital rate setting, and Certificate of Need — all of which failed miserably and caused enormous destruction in America's health care system.

One might think that, given this dismal track record, the command-and-control social planners would take a moment and rethink their assumptions.

Hah! One would think that only if one had never met any of these people. Introspection and self-doubt are not among their characteristics.

No, no, no, they think. Our policy prescriptions were spot on, we simply didn't go far enough. There must be something else we didn't account for...what could it be?

The American Hospital Association (that was so supportive of Certificate of Need as a way of preventing competition) would supply the ready answer — uncompensated care!

Their argument: Hospitals were burdened by providing free care to deadbeats. No wonder all of the remedies had failed.

Never mind questioning the logic, such as why uncompensated care would cause hospital prices or hospital utilization to grow. Why should one lead to the other? Sure, hospital prices might be higher to cover those costs, but why would they continue to grow year after year?

41

Policy makers didn't know that answer, but they were happy enough to latch onto this new issue as the reason their previous remedies had failed.

Of course, the next question would be — why was there so much uncompensated care?

This mental process is captured in an **article in Health Affairs in 1984 by Gail Wilensky,** "Solving hospital uncompensated care: targeting the indigent and the uninsured."[22]

The article starts out by stating in the abstract:

> "Uncompensated hospital care is a growing problem facing federal and state legislators, hospitals and doctors, and, indeed, all of society."

But that is not what the article itself says. In the text, the article is not at all sure it is a "growing problem," and is puzzled over what standard to use as a "deflator in constructing the time series estimate." If CPI is used, there is one result, if GNP is used it is another, and if hospital prices are used, yet a third. In the latter case, uncompensated care rose from $5.2 billion in 1978 to $6.2 billion in 1982 — hardly a crisis.

Indeed, the article says quite explicitly, "The amount of dollars spent on uncompensated hospital care is surprisingly small" — about 5% of hospital charges or 6% of hospital payments.
It further says, "Little is known directly about the characteristics of individuals who receive care for which the provider is not compensated." So, it is a tiny "problem" that is barely growing, and caused by people we know nothing about. Sort of a dead end, eh?

---

[22] http://content.healthaffairs.org/content/3/4/50.full.pdf+html?sid=3efb9197-1a0a-4817-b460-78fe08ae4ea3

Myth Busters

Not so fast. There is something we know a lot about:

> "We do, however, have information available about the types of hospitals that experience uncompensated care, such as the urban public teaching hospitals, other teaching hospitals, and, to a lesser extent, the voluntary hospitals and proprietary hospitals. Both the Sloan study and The Urban Institute study have indicated that hospitals with high concentrations of uncompensated care have disproportionate numbers of patients who are uninsured and low income."

And here comes the great pivot — switching from worrying about one issue — uncompensated care — to an entirely different one — the uninsured.

Dr. Wilensky had already been writing about the uninsured. The year before her uncompensated care article came out in 1984, she had another piece published in Health Affairs on "**Poor, Sick, and Uninsured,**" [23] in which she looked at expanding Medicaid to cover the approximately 1.4 million people who were uninsured for the entire year, low income, and in poor health according to 1977 data. She estimated that this population had doubled due to the recession in the early 1980s. Here is another example of using temporary economic conditions as a reason to create a permanent program.

So the new concern about uncompensated care simply added another rationale for doing something she was already working on.

Our next chapter will be about how the uninsured grew into a gigantic issue, but here it's worth noting that while uncompensated care became one of the cornerstones of the uninsured argument, it was never in fact much of a problem.

Some years later (1997) a team of RAND corporation researchers updated the **uncompensated care issue** [24] and found it hadn't grown

---

[23] http://content.healthaffairs.org/content/2/2/91.full.pdf+html?sid=ba805193-9469-4828-a1fc-ad870f617379

at all since the Wilensky article in 1984. It was about 6% of hospital costs in the 1984 article, and was still about 6% in the 1997 article. It had grown a bit (to 6.3%) in 1986, but had dropped back to 6.1% or $17.5 billion in 1995.

Look, this is a trivial amount of money. Retailers lose double that amount ($33.2 billion) to shoplifters every year, according to the CrimeDoctor Web site. [25]

In a free society some people take advantage of that freedom. In every sector business owners know that will happen and build the losses into their business models as a cost of doing business. Only in health care does it become a NATIONAL CRISIS worthy of federal intervention.

---

[24] http://content.healthaffairs.org/content/16/4/223.full.pdf+html?sid=0861ea75-991b-405a-ae84-008a7dd4da76
[25] http://www.crimedoctor.com/shoplifting-facts.htm

Myth Busters #9: Hysteria Over the Uninsured

After years of trying to do something about health care costs, especially hospital costs, through programs like National Health Planning, Certificate of Need, and Hospital Price Controls, the "health policy community" discovered the problem of Uncompensated Care. This, in turn, led to the discovery of The Uninsured — presumably the cause of Uncompensated Care (we are using proper nouns because these issues all quickly morphed from mere descriptions into titles for Great National Emergencies, like World War Two or the Great Depression).

This was a breakthrough. Here at last was an issue that would keep all the health policy wonks employed for a very long time. It is an issue that can never be solved! It can be converted into an annual CRISIS as each year the Census Bureau came out with new numbers and a new excuse to create new hysteria.

But, as the chart below shows, it has been about as stable a problem as anything could be. From 1987 through 2010 the proportion of the insured and uninsured had barely budged from roughly 84% insured and 16% uninsured. It has stayed the same during several recessions and during boom times. It has stayed the same despite massive efforts by state and local governments to expand Medicaid, reform the insurance market, develop (and abandon) all kinds of "universal healthcare" programs, and grow new federal programs like S-CHIP.

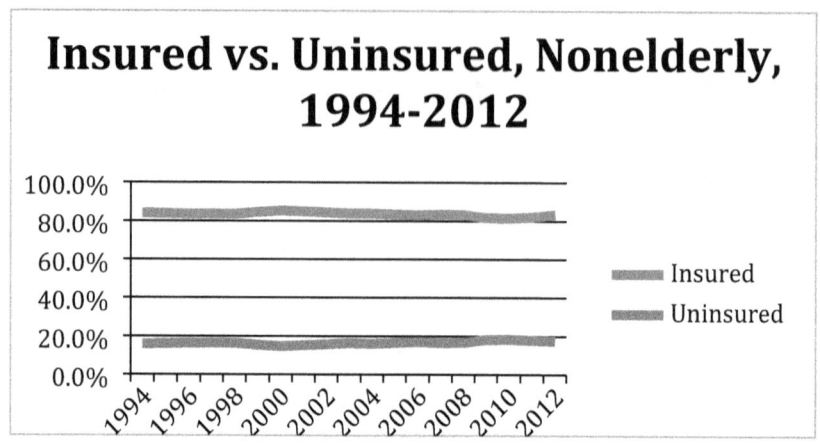

Source: U.S. Census Bureau Historical Tables [26]

Actually, this whole dichotomy — that there is one group of Americans who are insured and another group who are uninsured — is false.

In fact, the American economy is dynamic, fluid, and diverse — and so is the uninsured population. This is beyond the comprehension of most of the academic elite, which wants to place everything in tidy little boxes.

Americans change jobs all the time. They have part time jobs, they are independent contractors, they work on commissions, they will take several jobs at the same time, they supplement their income by selling Avon or restoring houses in their spare time, they move from town to town and state to state, they will take six months off between jobs to go to school or travel to Europe, they live off their savings, or sponge off girlfriends and boyfriends, they engage in barter, they win lawsuits or a lottery, they receive a substantial inheritance. To the extent health insurance is job-based, it will always be "unstable." It will come and go along with the jobs.

---

[26] http://www.census.gov/hhes/www/hlthins/data/historical/orghihistt1.html (1987 – 2004)
http://www.census.gov/hhes/www/hlthins/data/historical/files/hihistt1B.xls (2005-2010)

Myth Busters

Health insurance, too, is diverse. Some policies are very rich; others are skimpy; some (like Medicaid) are rich on paper but pay physicians so little that it is difficult to get services. The people who are least likely to have health insurance are young adults in their 20s. These are also the people who are least likely to need health care services. They are also the people who are least able to afford insurance premiums since they are just starting out in their careers or change jobs frequently while deciding what they want to do in life.

None of this is bad. In fact, it is good because it is a reflection of the real needs and priorities of real people. It is an appropriate allocation of their scarce resources. Even "uninsured" young adults are likely to be insured for the things most likely to happen to them — traffic accidents and work place injuries. Young women, who may need more health services than young men, are **far more likely to have it.** [27] In 2010, at age 21 to 24, 35% of men were uninsured, compared to 28.8% of women. At age 25 to 34 it was 30.2% of men and 21.7% of women.

In fact, no one is insured for everything. In that sense, we are all partially uninsured. There is nothing wrong with that. Even people who are well-insured may not be able to get health services when they need them. The point of having insurance is not to have a card in your wallet, but to finance needed health services. Health insurance finances these services on a prepaid basis — we pay a little bit ahead of time every month so that the insurance company will pay the bill when it is incurred.

That is one legitimate way to finance the services, but it is not the only way and may not be the best way. It is every bit as legitimate to incur the bill and finance it through a credit card or bank loan. That loan is paid off in monthly increments after the service has been received.

---

[27] Paul Fronstin, "Sources of Health Insurance and Characteristics of the Uninsured" Analysis of the March 2010 Current Population Survey," Employee Benefits Research Institute, September, 2010.
https://www.ebri.org/pdf/briefspdf/EBRI_IB_09-2010_No347_Uninsured1.pdf

Health Care Sharing Ministries offer yet another way. Members of the ministry all pitch in on a voluntary basis to pay the bills of other members who incur expenses.

Using health insurance is like a lay-away program at K-Mart. It is fine as far as it goes, but imagine trying to finance a car or a home that way. For those kinds of big purchases a bank loan is far more useful. Taking out a loan to finance expensive care will result in finance charges. But with pre-payment, one loses the value of the money while K-Mart (or the insurance company) holds on to it and adds their own administrative charges for managing the money.

For those reasons, it is actually more efficient to simply pay cash at the time of service whenever possible. One saves the financing cost of post-payment, and one saves the administrative and lost opportunity cost of pre-payment.

So, insurance has a role to play to health care financing, but it is foolish to think that it should have the sole or even primary role.

Myth Busters #10: Risk Pooling

In terms of the evolution of public policy, the "health policy community" failed at health planning, failed at hospital rate setting, failed at Certificate of Need, and failed to do anything about uncompensated care.

Not only had it failed, but it spent fortunes and destroyed lives in the process.

Then the same people turned their attention to the uninsured. I mean literally, the exact same people. The people who were unable to tell hospitals what facilities should be built or how much to charge for their services decided they could reorganize the insurance business. Hubris? Ya think?

This opened up a whole new world for them. Suddenly they had to learn some of that insurance lingo so they could sound like they knew what they were talking about. Suddenly health policy academics were buzzing with terminology like "risk pooling" and "adverse selection." Unfortunately, they couldn't quite grasp the meaning of the terms.

Take risk pooling. These health policy elites use the expression "risk pool" in two contradictory ways. Both are wrong.

First, they think of it as a giant pool of unallocated money everyone contributes to, and withdraws from when they have a need. They see it like taxes. Everybody pays taxes, which can then be fairly allocated based on each person's need (and the whim of the government.) Some people will have a lot of needs, others not so much, so we need lots and lots of people contributing to the pool so that no one person will have to pay too much. The bigger the pool, the better.

The other way they use it is to defend employer-sponsored health insurance over individual coverage. Employer coverage is better, they think, because it pools risk.

Let's start with the first one — the giant pool of money. This understanding places the emphasis on "pool" and ignores "risk." It leads to a "tragedy of the commons" phenomenon in which every member of the pool tries to grab as much as he can before it is depleted.

The emphasis should be on "risk." What is being pooled is the risk of a loss, an adverse event. The point is not to have a giant pool of money, but a pool of people (risks) large enough to cover expected losses. A risk is (and must be) an uncertainty. No one can know ahead of time who will incur a loss or when it will happen. But, it is possible to calculate the likelihood of losses for a large group of people, and divide that likelihood by the number of people covered to determine how much each should pay to cover these losses.

Each individual member of the group may have a higher or lower likelihood of incurring a loss and ideally there will be a mix of people to balance out the probabilities. Most insurance will assess each member's risk and adjust the premium to reflect that greater or lower risk. Obviously these rate adjustments do not account for all of the variation in risk or there would be no point in having the insurance in the first place. Most members of the pool will pay far more than they will collect in benefits, but we are willing to make that payment "just in case" something bad happens. Even with spending all that money, we would much prefer to never collect. It is far better to never be in a traffic accident or have your house burn down regardless of how much you pay for insurance.

Importantly, in this scenario there is no pool of unallocated money. Each dollar is contractually obligated to pay for a loss. We have a contract with the insurance company that we will pay $Y premium to get $X benefit in the event of a loss.

Myth Busters

Now, a risk pool does need a minimum of enrollees to be effective, but it is simply not true that the bigger the pool the better. Actuaries generally set the minimum number at 25,000 covered lives and place the optimal number at about 60,000. See, for instance, Elinor Hall, "MediCal Managed Care Models Context Considerations." [28]

This number provides all of the advantages of risk sharing that are possible. There may be some economies of scale in exceeding that number, but these, too, are limited. A study by the **World Bank** [29] **found** that the efficiency of any health insurance arrangement peaks at some number determined by both the size of the pool and the limits of managerial efficiencies. (See graph.)

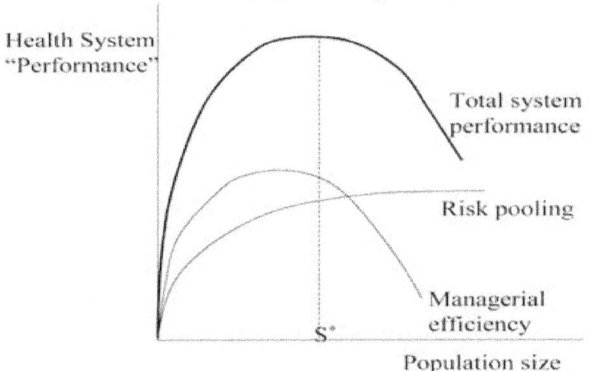

Figure 4: As population size increases, risk pooling performance improves: however managerial efficiency declines beyond a certain point. Optimal size is at S⁎

This raises the other use of the term that policy makers have been using — that employers are good vehicles for insurance coverage because they "pool risks."

28

http://www.dhcs.ca.gov/provgovpart/Documents/SPD%20Sonoma%20County-Report%20of%20the%20Planning%20Group%20on%20Medi-Cal%20Managed-Care.pdf

[29] Risk Pooling in Health Care Financing: The Implications for Health System Performance, Peter C. Smith and Sopie N. Witter, September 2004. http://siteresources.worldbank.org/HEALTHNUTRITIONANDPOPULATION/Resources/281627-1095698140167/Chap9SmithWitterRiskPoolingFinal.pdf

No they don't. Employers actually concentrate risk. A national employer with over 25,000 workers may be a reasonable risk pool, but the employees of a 75-person print shop are likely to be more like each other in their risks than like the general population. They work in the same place, live close to each other, are of similar ages, incomes, and education, and are exposed to the same environmental hazards. Further, they expose each other to the same diseases.

Employer-based coverage may have some marketing efficiencies over individual coverage, but it is the insurance company's job to be a risk pool, not the employer's.

Myth Busters #11: Mandated Benefits

As I said in the last chapter, the health policy community came to view risk pools as being a big pool of money to be allocated according to need. In that sense, there was little difference between insurance companies and government agencies. Both collected vast sums of money from a large number of people and spent it however their governing bodies determined.

The only problem, in this view, is that the governing bodies of insurance companies are unelected and unaccountable. They tend to be wealthy white males who are driven by greed and prejudice. Therefore, they deny benefits to certain classes of people — women, the mentally ill, the addicted. And they have little appreciation for the role of certain providers like nurses, psychologists, massage therapists, and so on.

It was, therefore necessary for state legislatures, or in some cases the Federal Congress, to intervene on behalf of those who needed protection from short-sighted insurance company executives.

Never mind that there was a contract in place, which was voluntarily entered into by the buyers and sellers of the insurance product. The contract said you pay us $X in premiums and we will provide Y benefit. The legislators decided that the contract should be revised to also provide Y+Z benefits.

Someone who is a better Constitutional scholar than I will have to explain whatever happened to the Contract Clause, which reads:

> "No State shall enter into any Treaty, Alliance, or Confederation; grant Letters of Marque and Reprisal; coin Money; emit Bills of Credit; make any Thing but gold and silver Coin a Tender in Payment of Debts; pass any Bill of Attainder, ex post facto Law, or Law impairing the Obligation of Contracts, or grant any Title of Nobility."

States are forbidden from "impairing the obligation of contracts." That seems pretty clear and unambiguous to me. Yet somehow states today have the authority to tear up existing contracts and add any provision they feel like.

That is a legal question, but there are also large political, economic, and policy issues at play here.

I won't go into the thousands of state mandated benefits currently in effect. The Council for Affordable Health Insurance has done a fine job of tracking these required benefits. [30]

Perhaps the biggest issue is the added cost of these mandates. In 1997, the National Center for Policy Analysis (NCPA) commissioned a study by the actuarial consulting firm, Milliman and Robertson (now just known as Milliman), entitled "**The Cost of Health Insurance Mandates,**" [31] which found the total number of mandates in effect at the time added as much as 30% to the cost of premiums. At the time, there were fewer than 1,000 such mandates on the books, and the most expensive ones were for mental health and fertility treatment, especially in vitro fertilization. Since then, over 1,000 more have been added, so the costs are proportionately that much higher.

Obviously, these requirements have made coverage less affordable for small employers and added greatly to the number of uninsured and the fall-off of coverage in the small group market.

But more than simple "affordability" is the perceived value of the coverage to the insurance buyer. Not many people will ever take advantage of in vitro fertilization coverage and a large segment could never benefit from it because they are beyond their childbearing years. It is of no conceivable (pun intended) value to

[30] Victoria Bunce and J.P. Wieske, "Health Insurance Mandates in the States, 2009" Council for Affordable Health Insurance.
https://www2.cbia.com/ieb/ag/CostOfCare/RisingCosts/CAHI_HealthInsuranceMandates2009.pdf
[31] John Goodman and Merrill Matthews, NCPA Brief Analysis #237, August 13, 1997. http://www.ncpa.org/pub/ba237

them. They may look at the price and the coverage and wonder why they should be expected to pay for something they are guaranteed to never use.

In that sense, these mandates are really hidden taxes, not insurance benefits at all. State government decides it would be good social policy to have someone pay for the fertility treatment of infertile couples, so it assesses a fee on a group of citizens who will never themselves benefit from the service. If you buy insurance coverage you are required to pay a tax that is dedicated to the treatment of a small number of people. The only option left for people who prefer not to pay that tax is to not purchase health insurance at all. So they don't, in large numbers.

State lawmakers had an opportunity to enact social policy on the cheap — at no direct cost to the taxpayers. And so they did, heedless of any consequences such as driving people to be uninsured. No one ever stopped to ask if it is worth depriving ten families of insurance coverage in order to provide free fertilization coverage to one. Insurance companies were viewed as giant cash cows. No one ever stopped to think that every penny an insurance company pays out comes from someone who pays premiums.

But mandated benefits never became a big political issue because only a small part of society was harmed by them — small employers, and to a lesser extent people who buy individual coverage. Bigger employers who self-fund their benefits were not subject to them because they are regulated by the federal ERISA law (the Employee Retirement and Income Security Act of 1974) – (see Chapter 17), which exempted them from any state laws "relating to" employee benefit plans. Large employers had no reason to resist the imposition of these mandates. If anything, they had plenty of reason to support them, because they added costs to their smaller-company competitors.

Naturally, with rising costs and greater complexity, consumers became increasingly angry at insurance companies. This has become an all too familiar bait and switch tactic with politicians.

They raise taxes or regulations on an industry, any industry – oil companies, auto makers, banks, drug companies – the companies increase their prices to pay for the new requirements (there is no other source), and consumers get mad at the industry for higher prices. Obamacare architect Jonathan Gruber recently got in trouble for speaking the truth – they were able to get by with raising taxes because they billed it as a tax on insurance companies when they knew perfectly well it was really a tax on people who buy insurance. He was amazed that people were gullible enough to think that somehow consumers would be exempt from the added cost. [32]

So, as mandated benefits drove up costs and made people angry at insurance companies, there were ever greater demands to "do something" to fix the problems in the insurance market. Next time we will look at how those efforts turned out.

---

[32] Greg Scandlen, "In Defense of Jonathan Gruber," The Federalist, December 14, 2014. http://thefederalist.com/2014/12/10/in-defense-of-jonathan-gruber/

Myth Busters #12: Universal Health Care

Before we dig deeper into insurance "reform" let's consider a detour some states took.

In just 15 years the focus of health policy moved from concern about rising hospital prices to the uninsured.

We began by trying to control the expansion of hospitals and moved on to trying to control hospital prices, to trying to address uncompensated care, all without a hint of success. The best efforts of the policy makers had no beneficial effect whatsoever. Yet these efforts cost many billions of dollars and likely damaged or killed thousands of patients. Yet no one was ever held to account. All were well paid for their efforts and all slept soundly at night thinking, "At least we tried to do something good."

Now they had discovered the uninsured and decided to apply their talents to fixing that problem. In earlier chapters I explained how these efforts also failed. In 1987, about 84% of the population had health insurance and 16% did not, as measured by the Current Population Survey of the Census Bureau. Twenty-three years later, in 2010, that ratio had barely budged. It has been about the flattest "trend" conceivable in human behavior.

Some of the policy people invested in this issue will argue that their efforts to expand insurance coverage is what kept the trend flat. Government programs have grown as private coverage has shrunk. It's actually far more likely to be the reverse — that, as government programs have grown, private coverage has shrunk because the (free) government coverage was available. This is known as "crowd-out." [33]

---

[33] Interestingly, one of the chroniclers of the "crowd out" phenomenon is Jonathan Gruber, who went on to become a key architect of the Affordable Care

The premise can be tested. If government programs expanded in response to shrinking private coverage there should be a lag time between the two, i.e. private coverage shrinks, the uninsured rise, then a couple of years later a new program comes on line to fill the gap and the numbers of uninsured drop again. There is no evidence for that. The very stability in the rate of the uninsured suggests the opposite.

In either case, if the goal was to reduce the numbers of uninsured, the policies have been yet another stark failure. And not for lack of trying — as with health planning a decade before, the entire health system was mobilized to implement the swell new ideas the policy community developed.

In the 1980s, as "the uninsured" became a discrete issue, the so-called policy community tended to go in two separate directions — universal health coverage or reform of the small employer market. We will look first at Universal Health.

Most of the advocates assumed there was little chance of getting universal health legislation enacted on the federal level with Ronald Reagan and then George H. W. Bush occupying the White House, so they took aim at the states.

Steffie Woolhandler, Benjamin Day, and David Himmelstein present a succinct history of the state efforts to enact universal health care in the **International Journal of Health Services.** [34]

It began in 1988 when aspiring presidential candidate and governor of Massachusetts Michael Dukakis got the legislature to enact a universal health care bill. He was quoted at the time as saying, "I am proud of the fact that Massachusetts will be the first state in the country to enact universal health insurance for all its citizens."

Act. He found that some 60% of enrollment in expanded public programs comes from people who were privately insured. See
https://www.nber.org/papers/w12858
[34]

http://www.pnhp.org/states_flatline/State%20Health%20Reform%20Flatlines%20IJHS%20-%202008.pdf

Myth Busters

The following year Oregon passed a similar law and governor Barbara Roberts crowed, "Today our dreams of providing effective and affordable health care to all Oregonians has come true."

In 1992, three states, Minnesota, Tennessee and Vermont all passed sweeping legislation that was widely heralded as parting the seas to Nirvana. The New York Times characterized Minnesota's law as, "the most sweeping effort yet to provide health insurance to people who lack it." Tennessee's governor, Ned McWherter, promised the state would cover "at least 95% of its citizens with health insurance by the end of 1994." Vermont governor Howard Dean promised universal coverage by 1995, saying "this is an incredibly exciting moment that should make all Vermonters proud."

Now, we expect empty promises and hyperbole from politicians, but what about the news media and "objective" analysts who are supposed to counter-balance political hype? Looking back on the coverage of the time, **Benjamin Day reflected in 2009:** [35]

> "Articles by our most respected news organizations hailed state reform after state reform as pioneering, likely to serve as models for the nation, and designed to control costs and extend health coverage to the uninsured. No reasonable reader of the news available at the time these laws were passed would expect that they might fail entirely to reduce the uninsured over time, or that they might not succeed in controlling costs at all."

He goes on to cite specific examples of major media outlets that were at least as enthusiastic about the new laws as their political sponsors were. Mr. Day observes that the media coverage was often devoted to the politics of the reforms, but indifferent to the economic viability of the ideas. This was especially true when there was bipartisan support for the ideas, as there often was.

---

[35] http://www.pnhp.org/news/2009/april/why-has-the-press-failed-us-in-reporting-on-health-care-reform

But, as it turned out, not one of these laws worked as promised. In some cases they slightly reduced the number of uninsured for a couple of years, mostly by expanding Medicaid, but the effect soon evaporated, partly because they did nothing to control costs. All of the laws were soon repealed.

The next chapter will look at small group reforms.

Myth Busters #13: Small Group Reform

Policy makers discovered the great fun of controlling insurance companies. There was so much money available and they could push social agendas without having to raise taxes! Plus, if things didn't work out it would be the insurance companies held to blame, not the policy makers. Sweet deal, indeed.

They could make the insurance companies pay for social programs such as treating alcoholics, the mentally ill, infertile couples. They could throw money at politically popular professions like psychiatric social workers, nurse midwives, dieticians, nutritionists — you name it. What fun!

Of course, there was one small problem. Health care costs were soaring in the late 1980s, the mandates added even more to the rising costs, and those nasty insurance companies loved to discriminate against people with problems. That wasn't fair, and the universal health programs passed by several states didn't work out very well. So, we have to DO SOMETHING to fix the new problems we created.

Now there was a rush at the state level to better control, not just the benefits offered, but the way these companies did business. These issues included underwriting practices, rating methodologies, marketing activities, and a host of other concerns such as how reserves are invested and how contracts are written.

It is doubtful that any other industry has been subject to this level of micro-management. Even utility regulation generally sets prices but doesn't get involved with the internal management decisions of the companies.

This is the consequence of the political class coming to see health insurers as quasi-social welfare organizations. The companies may be privately owned, but should operate like government agencies.

The National Association of Insurance Commissioners (NAIC) decided it had to step in and try to shape the new regulatory fervor. It launched a major initiative around small group reform in the late 1980s. This was a welcomed step by most of the industry. Yes, they would be much more tightly regulated, but at least it would be done by people who actually knew something about the business of insurance.

The NAIC was pretty realistic about what it could achieve. It knew very well it couldn't do much about lowering costs – these were determined by broader trends in the health care system. It might be able to help with access to coverage, but mostly it focused on "stability" in the small group market.

It developed several model acts to guide the states in reforming their markets. Since ERISA prohibits the states from regulating employer health plans, they were confined to the fully insured part of the market — which is mainly small group insurance. In a memo releasing two of these proposals, then-NAIC president Jim Long said the goals were:

- Assuring that coverage is made available to all small businesses, regardless of the health status or claims experience of their workers.
- Incorporating limits on abusive rating and renewal practices currently used by some insurers, and
- Providing continuity of coverage for insured small businesses changing carriers and for insured employees changing jobs.

An NAIC advisory committee noted that:

> "(These) reform measures are not intended to address the underlying problem of high health care costs – the most

frequent reason small employers give for not having health insurance. By bringing high-risk small employers and individuals in groups into the system, the committee believes that the reforms may in fact add to the cost of coverage for some small employers, especially for healthier groups." [36]

These proposals were aimed at spreading the added costs across the industry through some form of reinsurance or risk allocation mechanism, but few states adopted that approach. Most of them simply adopted the rating restrictions (limits on how much rates could vary based on age or health status) without including the cost-sharing aspects.

One consequence was a drastic consolidation of the industry as smaller insurance companies found it impossible to comply with the variations in state regulations, and did not have enough enrollment volume to absorb the added risk of the new regulations.

This consequence was fine with many regulators who had long complained that there was too much choice in the small group market, and that employers were confused by so many choices. They felt that the market would be better served with just three or four (maybe five) different carriers to choose from.

In this, they were incredibly successful. There is now a virtual oligopoly of sellers in the health insurance market, made up of the Blues, Aetna, Cigna, United, Humana, and sometimes Kaiser.

Next time we'll look at how some states adopted "reforms" that went astray.

---

[36] These NAIC documents are in my personal files. As far as I know they have never been published.

Greg Scandlen

Myth Busters #14: Insurance Reform Goes Crazy

While the National Association of Insurance Commissioners (NAIC) was rolling out a set of model laws for the states to consider in reforming their **small group insurance laws,** a handful of states decided to go much, much, further.

The NAIC models were focused on keeping the market working while ensuring access to coverage and preventing excessive rating variations between groups. It also proposed two alternative forms of risk sharing between carriers so no one insurance company would be hit too hard by a surge of high-risk enrollees. Almost all of the states adopted some variation of the rating restrictions but none adopted the risk-sharing provisions. A few years later the federal government adopted its own version of these requirements by enacting the Health Insurance Portability and Accountability Act of 1996 (HIPAA). These laws would go on to severely damage the market for small group coverage throughout the United States.

Meanwhile, a few states went well beyond these requirements and decided to apply even more onerous restrictions to both the individual (non-group) and small employer markets. New Jersey, New York, Maine, Massachusetts, Vermont, Connecticut, Washington, and Oregon all applied "community rating" to one or both market segments, along with "guaranteed issue" of some form.

Community rating means that all enrollees are charged the same premium regardless of their risk factors, and *guaranteed issue* means that all applicants must be accepted for coverage whenever they apply. In some cases the states also adopted a limited number of allowable standardized benefit plans.

Economists of every political persuasion warned these states that such restrictions cannot work in a voluntary market. At a minimum they will discourage the young and healthy from enrolling until they know they will need services, which will spur a "death spiral" of decreasing enrollment and ever-higher premiums. Liberal economists concluded that enrollment should therefore be mandatory, while conservative economists concluded that the restrictions should not be adopted at all. But both sides agreed that combining voluntary enrollment with these restrictions would doom the market.

But most of the politicians and "consumer advocates" in these states had no interest in listening. They were in such a fever to "do something" that reason was thrown out the window. It may also be possible that some of them did understand the consequences and knowingly adopted the restrictions anyway, thinking that the sooner the private market was destroyed, the sooner they would realize their real dream of a government-run health care system.

The late Conrad Meier of the Heartland Institute did a nice job of summarizing the experience of all eight states in a 2005 publication, "Destroying Insurance Markets." [37] This publication describes the precise experience of each state. He quotes the Council for Affordable Health Insurance (CAHI) from 1993 as warning against this approach to insurance regulation:

> "Most of today's uninsured are young and do not have much money. Community rating forces them to subsidize the cost of the middle-aged, who are at their peak earning power. Forcing the young to pay more will drive them out of the insurance market, raising costs for everyone."

Meier went on to look at what had happened ten years later and found that:

---

[37] https://www.heartland.org/publications-resources/publications/destroying-insurance-markets

Myth Busters

- Between1994 and 2003, the share of the population in these eight guaranteed issue states covered by individual health insurance plans fell dramatically.
- The eight states have seen a massive exodus of private insurance companies that had been selling individual health insurance policies.
- Premiums for individual insurance have soared.
- By contrast, states that did not adopt guaranteed issue and/or community rating have seen much smaller premium increases.

Meier took a closer look at each state, but we will confine our examination here to New Jersey, the poster child of these changes. He focused on three issues: rising premiums, declining coverage, and abandonment of the state by carriers.

Ten years after the reforms went into effect the rising cost of coverage was jaw dropping. For instance, Aetna's Plan "D" family premium went from $769/mo. in 1992 to $6,025/mo. in 2005. The increase for the New Jersey Blues was similar. These are neither the worst nor the best examples. Plan "D" is a fairly rich benefit design, but not outrageously so, with a $500 deductible and 80/20 coinsurance. Meier reported that in 2005 the lowest monthly premium for single coverage for each of the five plan designs was:

PLAN	DEDUCTIBLE	CARRIER	PREMIUM
Plan A	$1,000	Oxford	$517/mo.
Plan B	$1,000	Aetna	$756/mo.
Plan C	$1,000	Oxford PPO	$468/mo.
Plan D	$ 500	Oxford	$1,371/mo.
HMO	$ 15 copay	BCBS NJ	$494/mo.

Source: "Destroying Insurance Markets"

It is worth noting here that in states without community rating a 24-year old male would likely be charged under $100/mo. for coverage like this.

The number of people covered by individual coverage in New Jersey dropped dramatically, though the count varies considerably depending on who is doing the counting. Meier reports that the U.S. Census Bureau counted 998,000 people with non-group coverage in 1994 and 623,000 in 2003. The Employee Benefits Research Institute put it at 500,000 in 1992 and 300,000 between 2001 and 2003, while the state of New Jersey said coverage fell from 156,565 in 1993 to 78,298 in 2003. In all three cases enrollment fell substantially after the reforms were enacted.

In an **article in Health Affairs** in 2004, [38] Alan Monheit and colleagues confirm these assessments, writing that, "despite positive early evaluations, the IHCP (New Jersey's individual market) appears to be heading for collapse."

The "positive early evaluation" Monheit refers to is an article by Katherine Swartz and Deborah Garnick written in 1999 and cited in the Monheit article that was gushing in its praise for the program, calling it an "unprecedented achievement." To be generous, perhaps Swartz looked at it too early, before the perverse effects had really kicked in. But for years later the "policy community" kept citing the Swartz paper as proof that New Jersey was working just fine and those of us who predicted otherwise were delusional.

But Swartz was wrong. Monheit writes:

> "The IHCP's current situation points to a market that is heading for collapse. Enrollment has declined from a peak of 186,130 lives at the end of 1995 to 84,968 at the end of 2001. In addition, premiums have increased two- to threefold above their early levels. These changes have

---

[38] http://content.healthaffairs.org/content/23/4/167.full

raised concerns as to whether a comprehensive regulatory effort such as the IHCP can yield a sustainable health insurance market."

The reasons are obvious to anyone not blinded by a political agenda:

"Since pure community rating imposes the same premium on low- and high-risk people, the premiums of low risks exceed their actuarially fair level, while those of high risks are lower than their fair level. A sustainable market equilibrium may be tenuous under such a requirement."

Monheit also points out that the small group market was relatively healthy during this period, in part because New Jersey was enjoying economic growth (and job creation) and because the Small Employer Health Benefits Program, which was implemented about the same time, allowed for greater rate variation based on age and location. Indeed, while premiums in the individual market more than doubled from 1996 to 2000, small employer insurance grew only 30%. So enrollment in this segment grew from 694,312 in 2004 to 937,784 by the third quarter of 1999, before dropping again to 884,104 in the third quarter of 2001.

New Jersey eventually dropped its pure community rating requirement in the individual market, but one is left to wonder how many families were financially destroyed in the meantime by this misguided social experiment. How many people found they could no longer afford coverage and were thrown into the mercies of the charitable system? How many people continued to pay politically inflated premiums and were forced to curtail other important services?

No one ever bothers to count the people damaged by liberal social engineering. So people like Katherine Swartz continue to sleep well at night, heedless of the damage she has caused.

Greg Scandlen

Myth Busters #15: Adverse Selection

Another misunderstood principle of insurance financing is so-called "adverse selection."

This term is misunderstood or misapplied by most of the health policy community, which is poorly informed about insurance principles. The actual term is simply "selection." In a competitive market there is both anti-selection and pro-selection. A company that attracts the good risks is enjoying favorable selection, while one that attracts the poor risks is suffering negative (adverse) selection.

In either case, people who have a choice will select the company and the benefits that are most appropriate to their needs. An older person with back problems may load up on chiropractic benefits, while a young couple might prefer maternity coverage. In general, people of higher risk are much more likely to value and demand generous health insurance coverage while people of lower risk will place less value on it.

This principle can be used to support two very opposing responses. Each has profound consequences.

The first is risk-based rating, i.e., vary premiums according to the likelihood of use. Since some people value the coverage more, it is fair to charge them more, but since other people place a lesser value on the coverage it is necessary (and fair) to charge them less. Plus, it is possible to vary benefits according to each person's preference, so the older person doesn't pay for maternity and the younger couple doesn't pay for chiropractors. This is why, at least in the individual market, insurance is often sold with optional riders for services like prescription drug coverage, maternity, and visual and dental. Many people don't think they will ever use these services and don't want to pay for them.

An alternative response would be to eliminate choice by requiring all to have the same coverage. Require older persons to pay for maternity coverage even though they will not use the benefits and require the young couples to pay for chiropractic coverage even though they, too, will not use it. This approach spreads the cost of the benefits over a broader population, but it also risks creating resentment as people are forced to pay for services they know they will never use. Also, unlike the previous approach it causes some people to be over-charged and others to be under-charged. In general, those who are under-charged will over-insure — by purchasing more coverage than they otherwise would — while those who are over-charged will under-insure.

This second response also creates another problem, which is almost always overlooked in policy circles — moral hazard.

While selection means people will choose the benefits they are most likely to use, moral hazard means the opposite — once people are covered for something, they are more likely to use it. If I am required to be covered for psychiatric counseling, I am far more likely to make use of it, even if I would never use it otherwise. After all, I've already paid for it so why not use it?

Moral hazard applies to most of what insurance covers. Granted, the rate of maternity or traumatic injury may not be affected by moral hazard, but most outpatient and diagnostic services are. This is part of the reason so much of what is done in health care is considered non-essential. Having coverage leads to greater use of both essential and non-essential services.

It is also why the cost projections of expanding coverage are almost always underestimated. Budget analysts often assume that the behavior of a newly covered population will be constant — low users of the system will continue to be low users, or at most will consume services at the same rate as an already-covered population. But that fails to account for the pent-up demand question. Moral hazard suggests that newly insured people will consume more services when the cost of doing so falls.

Myth Busters

Both selection and moral hazard suggest the value in minimizing the amount of services that are paid through an insurance mechanism. Insurance is important to cover services that would otherwise be unaffordable, but the presence of insurance coverage changes behavior and distorts normal market mechanisms.

While we're on the subject, there is one other principle that should be mentioned. The surge in spending may not show up in the first year of coverage. It generally takes newly insured people about a year to figure out how to use their coverage. Also, benefits may not become available immediately. There may be an "exclusionary period" of 6 to 12 months for pre-existing conditions. The federal HIPAA law, for example, allows insurers to not pay benefits for conditions that existed prior to coverage for a period of 12 months. This phenomenon was part of the reason carriers used "durational rating" in which the first year's premium was lower than in succeeding years. Durational rating has been largely eliminated as consumer advocates viewed it as a bait and switch tactic, but the reality of lower first-year spending remains.

To sum up, selection means that people will choose the benefits they most prefer. Eliminating selection means forcing people to buy coverage they don't want and/or underpricing coverage they do want. In either case, people respond by obtaining the wrong amount of insurance — they over-insure or under-insure. Moreover, once they have benefits they would not have otherwise purchased, they will consume services they would not have otherwise consumed.

Eliminating "adverse selection" will always result in higher costs and dissatisfied consumers.

Greg Scandlen

Interlude: What Have We Learned So Far?

In the course of a mere twenty years — from the early 1970s to the early 1990s — public policy whipsawed the American health care system endlessly back and forth at enormous cost in dollars and lives and no noticeable benefit.

It began with a massive **national system of health planning** designed to do precisely the wrong thing — reduce services at a time of growing demand due to the advent of Medicare and Medicaid. This was predicated on a bumper sticker slogan, **"A Built Bed is a Filled Bed,"** that was certifiably wrong both in theory and in practice. Health planning failed and was soon repealed.

Then we moved on to all-payer **hospital rate setting** at the state level that was adopted by thirty states despite the lack of evidence that it could work in anything but the highest cost locations. These, too, were repealed in all but one state (Maryland) because the regulations were "incomprehensible" according to one supporter, and failed to work.

But most states retained some form of **Certificate of Need regulations,** which even the Department of Justice and Federal Trade Commission said failed to contain costs and were seriously anti-competitive. But that is exactly why the American Hospital Association supported these laws — they did not want to risk having to compete against more efficient rivals.

Then large employers got behind **"business coalitions on health"** that were based on the idea that sharp-penciled business executives could make doctors practice medicine more efficiently. Ultimately these efforts simply added yet another level of bureaucracy to a system that was already for too bureaucratic and did little to solve the problems of efficiency or cost.

Then the "policy community" discovered the "problem" of **uncompensated care.** After endless fretting and worrying about this new crisis, nothing happened and the level of uncompensated care, which was always a trivial amount of money, did not change a whit. When first discovered uncompensated care accounted for 6% of hospital costs and 13 years later it was still only 6% of hospital costs.

But the discovery of Uncompensated Care led to another discovery — **the uninsured.** Now here was an issue that would keep the policy community well-employed for decades and be the rationale for an entire bevy of new programs and initiatives. Yet over the course of the next two decades the level of non-insurance barely changed, in spite of all those programs. When it was first measured in 1987 about 84% of the population was insured and 16% uninsured. Twenty years later it was still 84% and 16%.

Of course, to effectively discuss the problem of the uninsured, policy makers would have to know something about insurance. Unfortunately, they learned just enough of the terminology to be dangerous. They completely misunderstood the meaning of ideas such as "**risk pooling**" and "**adverse selection.**"

But they had all the information they thought they needed to tell insurance companies how to run their businesses. They began by endorsing "**mandated benefits,**" which substituted the judgment of politicians for the buyers and sellers of health insurance in deciding what should and should not be covered in a health insurance policy. Over time over 2,000 specific laws would be enacted by the states. These laws did a lot to raise the price of coverage and make insurance less affordable, but the politicians were never blamed for these added costs. Only insurance companies were blamed.

Myth Busters

But mandates did not address the "great problem" of the uninsured, so some progressive states went further. They adopted **universal health programs** of one sort or another. These programs were adopted with great fanfare by politicians and hailed by publications like the New York Times as great breakthroughs. But one-by-one they all failed and were repealed. In some cases they were never actually implemented or in other cases were repealed only after much damage, but the only thing truly "universal" about them was failure.

Then the states set out to "reform" their insurance markets, and once again ended up not "reforming" them but destroying them. See the chapters on the NAIC **small group reforms** and the more ambitious individual market reforms in New Jersey and other states.

We haven't yet mentioned The Federal HMO Act or ERISA, which were also enacted in the 1970s, because these laws wouldn't have much impact on the market until the mid-1990s, but we will be getting to them in future chapters.

All of this was done in a mere twenty years. All of it failed, but only after creating much turmoil and doing real damage to the health care system, the economy, and the lives of families. It all adds up to the greatest experiment in social engineering of our lifetimes.

You may have noticed in this sorry saga that all of it was pushed by academics and politicians, and all of it was imposed upon hospitals, doctors, employers, and insurance companies. Who is missing? The patient/consumer/employee/taxpayer.

All of it was a clash between powerful elite interests who simply used concern for "the folks" as an excuse to gain power. Nobody in this story trusted the people to make their own decisions or control their own destinies.

The pretext of their activities was to control health care costs, improve health care quality, and ensure access to health care services. All of this effort failed to have any impact whatsoever on any of that. The nation would have been better served had none of this happened.

Myth Busters #16: How the Individual Mandate Came About

The controversy over past Republican support of an individual mandate needs some clarification. Many Republicans did indeed support this approach in the past. They proposed it as an alternative to what they saw as more onerous Democratic proposals for either single payer or an employer mandate.

There was an intense debate over the idea in conservative/libertarian circles and the libertarian perspective has won the argument. But this has been an honest and legitimate debate over an idea that had some merit but far more flaws. This is exactly the way public policy is supposed to proceed. No one should be ashamed of past support for the idea if they have learned from the process.

In our Myth Busters series we have gone from the early 1970s to the early 1990s — twenty years of catastrophic failure in public policy, at least in health policy. Every crazy idea was enacted into law, with large amounts of money appropriated, and the health system thrown into constant turmoil without any positive results whatsoever.

The social planners are nothing if not persistent, however. They concluded that the reason their previous efforts had failed was not because they were bad ideas, but that they were not comprehensive enough. If a bad idea fails on a small scale, the solution is, of course, to do the same thing on a gigantic, national scale.

In 1991, the Senate Democrats rolled out a proposal to require employers to either provide coverage or pay into a public program. This put Republicans on the defensive. They thought they, too, needed to "do something." *The Chicago Tribune* [39] at the time **wrote:**

"While Republicans praised the Democrats for taking the lead on changing health care, they took issue with details of the plan.

"Sen. Orrin Hatch (R-Utah), who has worked with Kennedy to develop many changes in health care, said the Democratic package contains "little or no flexibility for employers."

"Sen. John Chafee (R-R.I.) said Republicans hope to fashion a health-care reform package of their own in the next few weeks. Efforts to put together a bipartisan package fell apart several weeks ago, leaving each party on its own."

Republicans tend to be pro-business, so they didn't like the idea of an employer mandate, but they didn't like the idea of a public program, either. What to do? They came up with the idea of an individual mandate. This was widely supported by business groups who wanted the onus of a mandate taken off them. And if business likes it, then many Republicans will too.

It was given intellectual support by the Heritage Foundation, which thought the Federal Employees Health Benefits Program (FEHBP) was a model for how to organize the health insurance market.

Many libertarian groups vehemently disagreed with Heritage on this. John Goodman of NCPA, Ed Crane of Cato, and I, as then-CEO of the Council for Affordable Health Insurance (CAHI), all weighed in to urge Heritage to rethink its position.

Heritage had published a paper calling for the state of Maryland to enact such a mandate under the guise of "consumer choice." [40] But

[39] Elaine Povich, "Senate Democrats Unveil Health Plan," Chicago Tribune, June 6, 1991. http://articles.chicagotribune.com/1991-06-06/news/9102200296_1_health-care-reform-package-health-care-senate-democrats
[40] Bob Moffitt, "Why the Maryland Consumer Choice Health Plan could be a Model for Health Care Reform," Heritage Institute, June 12, 1992.

Myth Busters

I pointed out that the idea required so much regulation that it would virtually eliminate choice. Once the government mandates coverage, it has to define what benefits will fulfill the mandate, then it has to subsidize the people who cannot afford to comply, then it has to raise taxes to pay for the subsidy, then it has to control the insurance companies to make sure they aren't over charging for the mandated coverage. All of these steps would come true with a vengeance twenty-five years later with the enactment of the Affordable Care Act

It is curious that using FEHBP as a model would lead to this result, since participation in FEHBP was not mandated. Federal employees remained free to get coverage elsewhere or to go without coverage at all.

A few years later, Mitt Romney's support for a mandate in Massachusetts was based on the fear that the Democrats in the legislature had the votes to enact a single payer system in the state. He (and Heritage) offered up the mandate as an alternative.

Other people liked the individual mandate as a way of getting employers out of the health insurance business. Some insurance groups simply liked the idea of making people buy what they were selling. Still others thought of it as a way of ensuring that people take "personal responsibility" for their actions. Some people thought a mandate would be good, but only under certain circumstances — like if it applied only to high deductible plans, say, or if people could opt-out by proving they could pay their own expenses. None of these positions are irrational. One can understand the thinking behind them, even while believing they are profoundly wrong.

If anything, this all shows a level of intellectual vitality in conservative circles that is missing on the progressive side of the spectrum. Over time the argument has been largely won by those of us who oppose mandates, and we have been helped by the stark reality of Obama's health care law. Suddenly it was not just an intellectual exercise but had become the law of the land.

But there are lessons to be learned here.

- Ideas have consequences. We shouldn't support something unless we are willing to live with the results.
- If we believe in the ability of markets to fix problems, we should not short circuit that process just because we are impatient.
- Politics is not just a debating society. Politics leads to the enactment of laws and laws require certain actions.
- Business can be parochial. It doesn't care about ideology or even economics. It just wants to make a profit. It will support government actions that it thinks will lead to greater profitability for itself even at the expense of liberty for others.
- Politicians like to have power and power is the ability to tell other people what to do. Very few politicians are able to resist exercising their power.

The big question for the policy community is, are we able to resist the temptation to "solve problems" by forcing people to do what we want them to do? Can we be humble enough to accept that people may make decisions for themselves that we think are misguided?

Ron Kessler provides more background on all this in a **NewsMax** article.[41]

---

[41] Ron Kessler, "GOP Leaders Backed a Healthcare Mandate" NewsMax, June 8, 2011. https://www.newsmax.com/RonaldKessler/Healthcaremandate-HeritageFoundation-Gingrich-Nixon/2011/06/08/id/399250/

Myth Busters #17: ERISA

We are almost up to 1992 in our history of health reform. So far we have dealt with:

- The fallacy of "Roemer's Law," which has driven most of these policy initiatives.
- How Roemer's Law often leads people to misunderstand events, such as by Jack Wennberg (Dartmouth Health Atlas) in his look at hysterectomies in Maine.
- The rise and fall of national health planning, also based on Roemer's Law.
- The rise and fall of hospital rate setting.
- The advent of Certificate of Need regulations, which are still on the books in most states.
- The formation of business coalitions on health.
- The discovery of uncompensated care.
- The hysteria over the uninsured.
- The misunderstanding of risk pooling.
- The growth of mandated benefits.
- The failed state efforts to create universal health insurance schemes.
- The efforts by the states to "reform" their small group markets.
- Insurance reform goes crazy.
- The misunderstanding of adverse selection.
- The idea of an individual mandate.

All of this in just 20 years (1972–1992). But we aren't quite done yet. There was another thing that happened in this period that had a profound effect on health care delivery and financing. This was the Employee Retirement and Security Act (ERISA) of 1974.

ERISA was enacted mostly because some recent corporate bankruptcies had left retirees with no income and no recourse. Among other things, it created the Pension Benefit Guaranty Corporation (PBGC), which was modeled after the state guaranty funds for insolvent insurance companies. [42] (Note: Because insurance companies are state regulated, federal bankruptcy laws do not apply to them. The states have developed other methods for dealing with insolvent insurance companies. I would argue these state remedies are far more effective and beneficial to policyholders than anything the federal government has done.)

That part of the law has worked reasonably well, it is ERISA's application to health coverage that has created far more problems than it ever solved.

One example would be that any plan governed by ERISA is exempt from all state taxes and regulations and that all legal challenges to employee benefit plans have to be filed in the federal courts. Congress wanted to ensure that the assets of such plans would not be diminished by legal judgments and state revenue demands. This might be appropriate for pension programs that rely on accumulated reserves to pay benefits decades in the future, but not for health benefits that are funded on a year-to-year basis.

Similarly, although ERISA provides a federal remedy for contract disputes, it confines judgments to the cost of the denied claim plus attorney's fees. Again, this may be fine for pension programs that merely provide income to a beneficiary, but in health care the failure to pay a claim can mean the worsening of a medical condition or even the death of a patient. There is no remedy for these situations because punitive damages or pain and suffering damages are not allowed.

Some people have looked at these provisions and concluded that Congress must not have really meant to include health benefits in

---

[42] Greg Scandlen, "Legislative Malpractice: Misdiagnosing Patients' Rights," Cato Institute, April 7, 2000. https://www.cato.org/publications/briefing-paper/legislative-malpractice-misdiagnosing-patients-rights

the scope of ERISA, but that isn't true. The law is very clear in defining an "employee welfare benefits plan" —

> "(A)ny plan, fund or program… established or maintained by an employer… for the purpose of providing for its participants or their beneficiaries, through the purchase of insurance or otherwise, medical, surgical… or hospital care or benefits, or benefits in the event of sickness, accident, disability, death, or unemployment." (29 U.S.C. Sect. 3(1))

What was really going on was that Congress expected that a federal program would shortly take over all health care financing, so it was not as diligent about the implications on health care of this law as it should have been. It is worth noting that the famous RAND Health Insurance Experiment (HIE) was done about the same time for the same reason. As a recent (2006) **research brief from RAND** [43] said:

> "In the early 1970s, financing and the impact of cost sharing took center stage in the national health care debate. At the time, the debate focused on free, universal health care and whether the benefits would justify the costs. To inform this debate, an interdisciplinary team of RAND researchers designed and carried out the HIE, one of the largest and most comprehensive social science experiments ever performed in the United States."

Obviously that did not happen, so we have been stuck with ERISA ever since.

It is doubtful there has ever been a law as widely misunderstood or as frequently litigated as ERISA. Few people at the time — or since — have appreciated the implications. In 1982 Paul Starr wrote a Pulitzer Prize winning book, *The Social Transformation of*

---

[43] Multiple authors, "The Health Insurance Experiment: A Classic RAND Study Speaks to the Current Health Care Reform Debate."
http://www.rand.org/health/feature/forty/health_insurance_experiment.html

American Medicine, that failed to even mention ERISA in any of it's 514 pages.

The U.S. Supreme Court issued almost annual decisions on ERISA through the 1980s, the most prominent being *Union Labor Life v. Pireno* (1982), *Shaw v. Delta Airlines* (1983), *Metropolitan v. Massachusetts* (1985), and *Pilot Life v. Dedeaux* (1987).

We need to delve pretty deeply into ERISA before we pass on to other topics. As we said, ERISA's application to health benefits was not thought through very well because Congress expected to pass a universal federal health system any day. Still, it would seem a tad more thought should have gone into writing the law.

Sadly, Congress and the rest of the federal government didn't know very much about insurance then (and now), so it had little idea what it was doing. Back in 1945, Congress had enacted the McCarran/Ferguson Act to restore the states as the sole regulators of the insurance industry. [44]

This is a story in itself. Insurance had never been considered "commerce" and so was exempt from federal involvement under the Commerce Clause until 1944 when the Supreme Court decided suddenly that it was indeed commerce in the *United States v. South-Eastern Underwriters* decision. [45] Here was yet another example of judicial activism. What had changed in 150 years to make something that never was "commerce" suddenly become commerce? *Stari decisis* seems to apply only to conservative opinions.

In any case, Congress quickly decided it wanted to have nothing to do with insurance regulation, so it enacted McCarran/Ferguson to kick that responsibility back to the states. So, Congress and the federal government generally have never been involved in

---

[44] "Antitrust Law and Insurance," Insurance Information Institute, http://www.iii.org/article/antitrust-law-and-insurance
[45] "United States v. South-Eastern Underwriters: 322 U.S. 533 (1944)," Justia U.S. Supreme Court. https://supreme.justia.com/cases/federal/us/322/533/

insurance regulation and have no expertise in the area. And it shows.

ERISA was Congress' attempt to regulate employer benefits plans without regulating insurance. The distinction is a three-step process:

The Preemption from State Law. This applies to all employers large and small (except church and government plans). All are exempt from any and all state laws and regulations that "relate to" employee benefit welfare plans.

The Savings Clause. This "saves" from preemption those laws that regulate the business of insurance — even when the insurance buyer is an employer.

The Deemer Provision. This "deems" that employers who provide benefits are not in the business of insurance.

Thus, all employers large and small are exempt from state regulations and taxes for the purposes of their health benefits, but insurance companies are not. So an employer who buys coverage from an insurance company is only indirectly affected because the insurer is regulated.

ERISA is hard to understand because it makes an irrational distinction between two virtually identical forms of health care financing: A) Health insurance that is bought from insurance companies and: B) Health insurance that is simply administered by those same insurance companies. There is no visible difference between the two. A consumer cannot know whether she has A or B; neither can a provider. Both plans provide the same identification card, both use the same process for filing claims, both cover pretty much the same services, both have the same appeals processes and the same customer services.

Even the distinction between employer-based coverage and other forms of coverage is opaque. Some employers self-fund their benefits, while others buy it from regulated insurance companies.

ERISA assumes the former are exempt from state law while the latter are not, but only because the insurers are not exempt. But in practice there are a host of arrangements that fall in between — partial self-funding, self-funding with a stop loss, self-funding with reinsurance.

Do you have a headache yet?

The rationale for ERISA was to allow multi-state employers to provide the same benefits to the employees in all states. But this is not what the law actually says. It does not confine itself to multi-state employers. Companies in just one state are also exempt from state law.

Besides, multi-state employers are subject to all kinds of varying state regulations — wage and hour laws, permitting requirements, building codes, environmental restrictions, taxes — and they seem to be able to cope with them. Why should health benefits be any different?

The fact that employers were exempt from state laws made them indifferent to the growing mountain of new laws and regulations the states enacted on health insurance during the 1980s. This tilted the balance of power in state legislatures and left only insurance companies and small employers to object to these proposals. Insurance companies are easy to revile and small employers don't have much political influence, so it was "Katy bar the door" and costs soared, leaving many people without coverage.

The effects have been profound. ERISA enormously advantaged employer-sponsored plans over individual coverage, and it virtually created the idea of employers' self-funding of benefits to escape state regulations. It also enraged citizens who found they could no longer seek reasonable compensation for damages caused by their health plans. This problem became especially acute when Managed Care began to take over the health benefits market. And this, too, was fomented by federal interference in the benefits market in the form of the Federal HMO Act, which we will get into next time.

But, once again, we have an example of Washington's policy elite screwing things up and escaping any responsibility for their actions. The insurance companies got blamed for rising prices and the politicians got off scot-free. What a way to run a country — or a health system.

Greg Scandlen

Myth Busters #18: The Federal HMO Act and Other Tinkering

In 1973, President Nixon secured passage of the Federal HMO Act.[46] He thought encouraging HMOs would help lower health care costs and deter demands for a national health program. The supposition was that moving to HMOs would replace fee-for-service payments with capitation models in which the plans were paid a fixed annual amount for each enrollee.

The law provided $375 million in seed money for federally qualified HMOs, and required employers with 25 or more employees to offer HMO coverage if one was available in their area. [47] To qualify as a federal HMO, a plan had to offer a certain array of benefits, community rate their premiums, provide quality assurance programs, and comply with a host of other restrictions on marketing, financial accounting, and enrollment practices. [48]

Despite, or because of, these federal advantages, HMO enrollment never really took off until this law was amended in 1988 to remove most of the restrictions. But a lot of other things had happened in the interim, including the adoption of hospital "Diagnosis Related Groups" (DRGs) in the Medicare program. The National Council on Disability reports –

> "Once the DRG system was fully phased in, Medicare payments to hospitals stabilized. However, since DRGs applied to inpatient hospital services only, many hospitals, like many group medical practices, began to expand their

---

[46] The Health Maintenance Act of 1973, P.L. 93-222.
[47] National Council on Disability, "A Brief History of Managed Care," 2013. http://www.ncd.gov/publications/2013/20130315/20130513_AppendixB
[48] Employee Benefits Research Institute (EBRI). https://www.ebri.org/pdf/publications/books/fundamentals/fund23.pdf

outpatient services in order to offset revenues lost as a result of shorter hospital stays. Between 1983 and 1991, the percentage of hospitals with outpatient care departments grew from 50 percent to 87 percent. Hospital revenues derived from outpatient services doubled over the period, reaching 25 percent of all revenues by 1992.

"Since DRGs were applied exclusively to Medicare payments, hospitals began to shift unreimbursed costs to private health insurance plans. As a result, average per employee health plan premiums doubled between 1984 and 1991, rising from $1,645 to $3,605. With health insurance costs eroding profits, many employers took aggressive steps to control health care expenditures. Plan benefits were reduced. Employees were required to pay a larger share of health insurance premiums. More and more employers—especially large corporations—decided to pay employee health costs directly rather than purchase health insurance. And a steadily increasing number of large and small businesses turned to managed health care plans in an attempt to rein in spiraling health care outlays.

So, in a classic game of "whack-a-mole," the federal government reduced payments for hospital in-patient care, and the hospitals responded by jacking up use of outpatient services and raising prices for employers.

Meanwhile, the HMO industry was transforming from mostly non-profit "staff models" where the plan owned facilities and paid doctors salaries, to "independent practice" (IPA) models that contract with hospitals and private practice physicians, and "preferred provider" (PPO) networks that pay physicians on a discounted fee-for-service basis. It also transformed from largely non-profit to investor-owned profit making corporations.

All of this was distressing to the early advocates of HMOs. In a review of the book "The Rise and Fall of HMOs," by Jan Gregoire

Coombs, [49] health economist Alain Enthoven quoted the book's author as saying –

> "The long awaited HMO Act of 1973 failed to resolve the nation's health care crisis and nearly derailed the HMO movement…. Subsequent federal and state legislation intended to facilitate prepaid health care often had the opposite effect. Federal funding gave prepaid health care a legitimacy long denied by the medical profession, but the federal requirements for HMOs deterred many potential sponsors."

Coombs and Enthoven both had high regard for Wisconsin's Marshfield Clinic, which had partnered with Blue Cross of Wisconsin and St. Joseph's Hospital to form the GMCHP HMO. This, they thought, was a model of how to do health care right. But, alas, Enthoven writes it was a story of how "one of the HMOs that struggled to remain true to its mission despite the market and political forces stacked against it (and) reveals a history of health reform gone wrong."

Well, actually, in any industry a business model that fails to align with "market and political forces" will, and should fail. It really doesn't (or shouldn't) matter what starry-eyed academics think about it. But the academic advocates of managed care never gave up. Like Communists who dismiss the failure of the Soviet Union because it wasn't done right, but believe next time it will work just fine, these academics learned nothing from the failure of managed care in the 1990s and inserted a new version in the form of "accountable care organizations" into the Affordable Care Act.

---

[49] Alain Enthoven, "The Rise and Fall of HMOs shows how a worthy idea went wrong,' Commonwealth Magazine, April 10, 2005.
http://commonwealthmagazine.org/arts-and-culture/emthe-rise-and-fall-of-hmosem-shows-how-a-worthy-idea-went-wrong/

Greg Scandlen

Myth Busters #19: Fee-For-Service is the Problem?

Almost everyone involved in health care will tell you that the greatest problem in our system is that we pay on a fee-for-service basis. Almost everyone is wrong.

The logic is obvious – paying a fee for a service encourages providers to get more fees by providing more services. Ergo, we consume too much and spend too much. Ipso facto, getting rid of fee-for-service would result in fewer services and less spending. Case closed.

Well, maybe not.

In fact, almost everything we do in the course of our economic lives, we do on a fee-for-service basis. When we go to the movies, get our oil changed, have our roof replaced, buy a computer, get a haircut, hire a baby sitter, buy a steak dinner, get someone to do our taxes or defend us in a suit, we do it on a fee-for-service basis. None of it is particularly inflationary.

The **graph** [50] below shows the CPI broken into components. Food, housing transportation, apparel – all are paid fee-for-service and all have a lower rate of inflation than health care.

---

[50] Doug Short, Advisor Perspectives, "What Inflation Means to You" January 18, 2017. https://www.advisorperspectives.com/dshort/updates/2017/01/18/what-inflation-means-to-you-inside-the-consumer-price-index

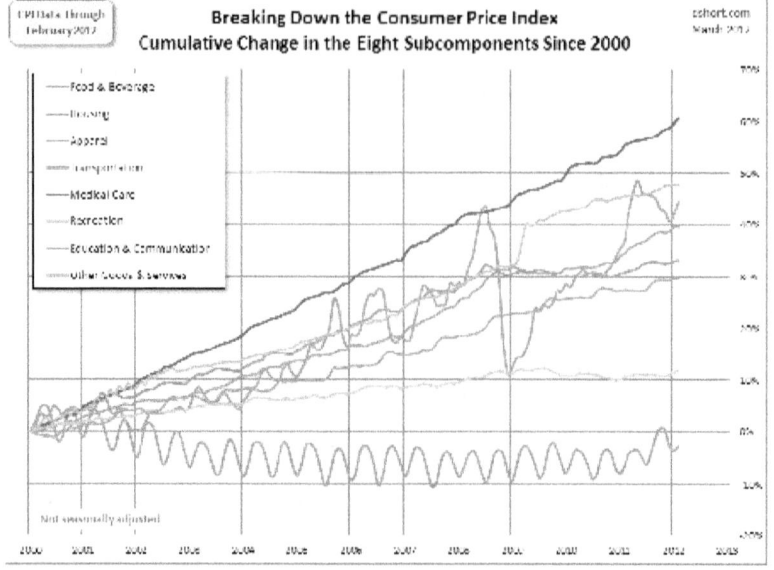

Breaking Down the Consumer Price Index
Cumulative Change in the Eight Subcomponents Since 2000

Yes, the providers of these services would like to sell us more units of service. But we have good reason to resist – we don't want to waste our money on services we don't need.

What is unique about health care is not fee-for-service, but third-party payment. Only in health care is there someone else picking up the tab for our spending.

If we applied the same third-party payment technique to any other segment of the economy we would get the exact same inflationary spiral we see in health care. I buy donuts from time-to-time. If those donuts were free at the point of purchase, I would buy (and eat) a whole lot more than I do today. The stereotype of cops eating donuts came about because the donut shops gave them away to the cops for free.

When I was working as a state-level lobbyist for the Blue Cross Blue Shield Association, I would attend meetings of the National Association of Insurance Commissioners (NAIC), the National Governors Association (NGA), the National Conference of State

Myth Busters

Legislators (NCSL) and a bunch of other organizations. These groups typically held their meetings in the ritziest hotel in Kansas City, New Orleans, San Diego, Boston or some other place that was easy to get to.

Never, not once, did I ever inquire what the room would cost when I checked in. Why should I? Blue Cross was paying for it. The cost made no difference to me whatsoever. Some years later when I went into business for myself and tried to attend the same meetings at my own expense, I became very interested in the cost of the rooms. Most of the time, I would stay at a cheap motel on the edge of town and drive to the meetings.

Ah, but health care is different, you might say. Yes it is. It is different because of third-party payment and for no other reason. The other reasons usually given are easily rebutted –

- Information asymmetry (the providers know more than the patients). Of course, but that is also true of, say, criminal law or engineering.
- Health care is essential to life. But it is far less essential than food or housing, which do not require third-party payment.
- Patients are too fearful to make rational decisions. More fearful than if I were arrested and locked up at Riker's Island?
- Health care is complicated. As complicated as an iPad? I don't think so.

Efforts to move away from fee-for-services or to control it never work very well. Witness capitation under managed care, or the RBRVS system of paying physicians under Medicare. Medicare's system of price controls leads to absurd complexity yet does not reward physicians for the things that are most important to patients, such as kindness, patience, communication ability, friendliness – the qualities that humanize the medical transaction and that would be rewarded in any other segment of the economy not dominated by bloodless third-party payers.

The recent adoption of the ICD-10 codebook has made it a whole lot worse. This offers 140,000 separate billing codes, according to **The Wall Street Journal,** [51] including separate "codes for injuries in opera houses, art galleries, squash courts, and nine locations in and around a mobile home, from the bathroom to the bedroom."

It is not fee-for-service that is the problem, but the burden third-party payers put on patients and providers alike, without adding any value whatsoever.

[51] Anna Wilde Matthews, "Walked Into a Lamppost? Hurt While Crocheting? Help Is on the Way," Wall Street Journal,   September 13, 2011. https://www.wsj.com/articles/SB10001424053111904103404576560742746021106

Myth Busters #20: Bundled Payments Are the Answer?

One of the more peculiar mental twists by the health academics is the notion that the answer to the problems with fee-for-service is to bundle some of these services into single packages.

As we argued in our last chapter, FFS is not a problem in health care or anywhere else. The problem is third-party payment. But for the moment let's suspend our disbelief and accept that FFS is a problem. In what way does bundling solve it? Or even address it?

The proponents of bundling would go from paying a fee for a single service to paying a fee for a bundle of services. It is still fee-for-service. In fact services are already bundled. An office visit to a doctor "bundles" many discrete services such as weighing the patient, getting a blood pressure reading, checking pulse and lungs, interviewing the patient about how she is feeling and whether she is having any reactions to the drugs that were prescribed during the last visit. These services are not billed separately but are "bundled" into an "office visit" package.

Presumably, the advocates of bundling would want more and bigger bundles, or they think they know what should be in the bundle better than the physician does. Or perhaps they have no idea what they are talking about -- it is simply the latest nifty sounding term they use to pretend they have something to say. If third-party payment encourages doctors to perform more services, would it not also encourage doctors to perform more bundles of services? Is there really any difference? Are there any examples in the real world of how bundling might actually work?

Well, yes, as the matter of fact. There is one very big sector of the economy that is all about bundling. That is higher education. When young people go off to school, they do not pay separate fees for different professors or different courses. They pay a single annual tuition that covers an entire year's instruction. The tuition is also "community rated." Other than a distinction between in-state and out-of-state, all students are charged the same rate. The smart ones pay the same as the dumb ones even though the two groups will require different levels of service. Everybody pays the same for a comprehensive bundle of services.

This is just perfect. It is everything an academic could hope for in health care. Surely higher education is a great example of these progressive principles in practice and a beacon for what we could do in health care

Well, maybe with one teensy exception. It doesn't slow spending a whit -- quite the opposite. Doug Short expands on the **CPI chart** [52] below to include "College Tuition & Fees" as a separate item.

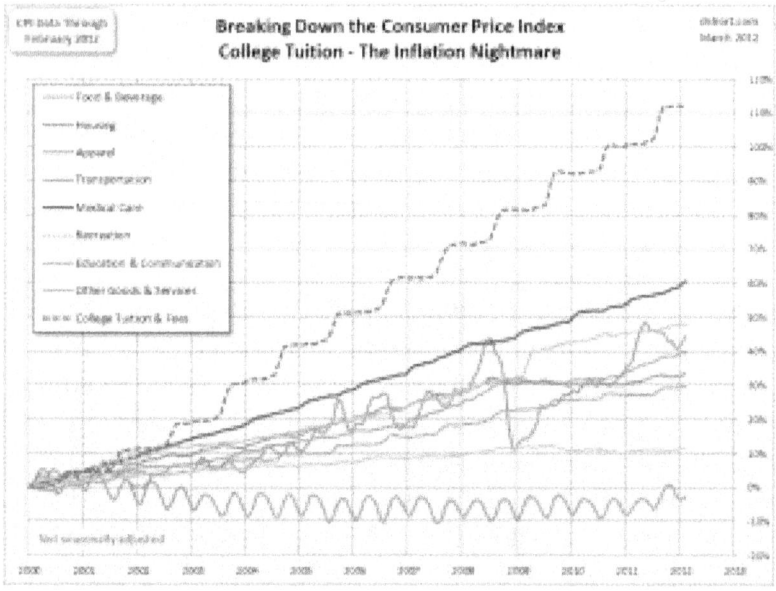

---

[52] Doug Short, Advisor Perspectives, "What Inflation Means to You" January 18, 2017. https://www.advisorperspectives.com/dshort/updates/2017/01/18/what-inflation-means-to-you-inside-the-consumer-price-index

Myth Busters

It turns out that college costs have risen twice as fast as even health care since 2000! It is unrelenting. Year after year, during good times and bad, it rises twice as fast as health care.

Is bundling a bad idea? Of course not. Physicians have been bundling for all eternity. They do it when it makes sense and enhances value. But today they are not allowed to create new bundles because the federal government doesn't pay that way. It pays according to discrete ICD codes that are getting increasingly (and absurdly) specific.

But neither is bundling a panacea, especially if it is dictated by the same people that brought us the ICD-10 codebook.

Two of the early advocates of bundling came to have second thoughts about it after a few years. They are James Caillouette, Surgeon-in-Chief at the Hoag Orthopedic Institute, and James Robinson, economics professor at UC Berkley, who write in **Health Affairs** [53] that –

> "As leaders in the Integrated Health Association (IHA) bundled payment initiative, we shared the same hopes, devoted the same energies, and share the same frustrations with the modest results. We feel it is important to emphasize what we consider to be the initiative's most important design failure: the lack of engagement and alignment on the part of the consumer. No one will ever reform the U.S. health care system without bringing the consumer along and, indeed, placing consumer choice and accountability at the very center of the reform initiative."

They go on –

---

[53] James Cailloette and James C. Robinson, "The Failure of Bundled Payment: The importance of Consumer Incentives," Health Affairs Blog, August 21, 2014. http://healthaffairs.org/blog/2014/08/21/the-failure-of-bundled-payment-the-importance-of-consumer-incentives/

"We were first and the most enthusiastic participant in IHA bundled payment initiative, sending the hospital's entire C-suite to the founding meeting with the health insurers. We signed more contracts and treated more patients than any other participant. But we never received the volume of new patients necessary to cover our incremental expenses, much less finance a much-desired expansion."

They conclude –

"Our policy focus right now, however, is in encouraging the alignment between consumers and providers through reference pricing, travel medicine, quality reporting, and price transparency."

Well, better late than never! These are precisely the remedies that many of us have been advocating for about 20 years now. But the "health policy community" keeps getting distracted by whiz-bang new slogans like ACOs, bundled payments, case management, and the latest — Big Data! None of these are actually new ideas. They are all just repackaging of the same old ideas that have failed in the past. They all involve some smart guys (or committees of smart guys) telling everybody else what to do.

But, maybe there is hope if even Health Affairs is publishing articles about the essential role of empowered and engaged consumers making good decisions.

Myth Buster #21: Third-Party Payment

No term is as widely misunderstood as "third-party payment." Most health policy people hear that expression and automatically think "insurance coverage." "My goodness," they think, "critics of third-party payment want to abolish all insurance! It's not even worth talking to them."

But this attitude is wrong. Third-Party Payment (TPP) has a specific and precise meaning. It is a form of coverage in which the payer (third party) pays a provider (second party) to deliver a service to a patient (first party).

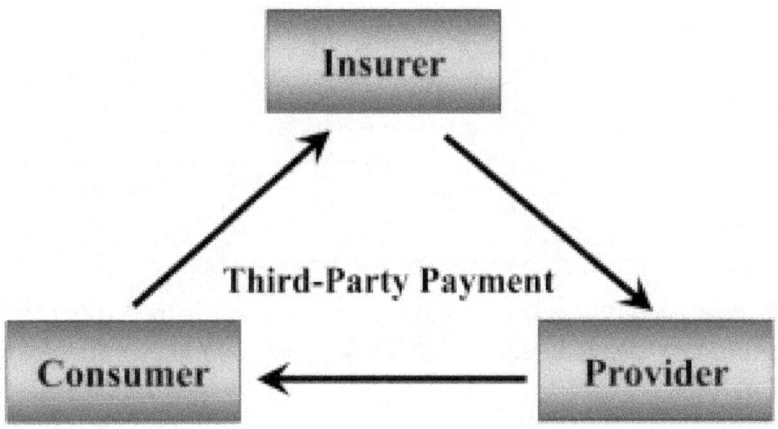

By contrast, most forms of insurance consist of a two-party contract. The first party (the consumer) buys a policy from the second party (the insurer). When the insured incurs a "loss" the insurer pays a benefit to the insured.

Third-party payment never existed until it was created by Blue Cross in the 1930s. Blue Cross was actually invented by the hospitals that were concerned about their financial condition during the Depression, which was dire. Paul Starr, in his book "The Social Transformation of American Medicine," wrote, "In just one year (after the crash of 1929) average hospital receipts per person fell from $236.12 to $59.26." Total national spending on health care fell from $3.6 billion in 1929 to $2.8 billion in 1935.[54] Hospitals were desperate to find a reliable source of revenue and came up with the idea of "pre-payment" – people would pay today for a stay in the hospital later on when they needed it.

The prototype was launched by Baylor Hospital in Dallas in 1929, and soon replicated by other hospitals around the country. The whole movement was endorsed by the American Hospital Association (AHA) in 1932, and actually absorbed into the AHA by 1939. [55]

For many years Blue Cross (and later Blue Shield) insisted it was not "insurance," but "prepaid hospital (or medical) service organizations." They were organized, not under state insurance laws, but under special enabling legislation in the states that provided them with special tax-exempt status and immunity from many of the regulations that apply to insurance companies. For instance, they were exempt from insurance reserve requirements because their hospital members guaranteed their solvency. They were set up as not-for-profit organizations and had Boards of Directors that were controlled by their hospital members. This would have been a flagrant antitrust violation but for the "state action" doctrine, which exempts state-regulated companies from anti-trust law.

Blue Cross strictly avoided insurance terminology, calling its customers "subscribers," rather than insureds, who paid "subscription fees" rather than premiums, and received "service benefits," rather than a monetary payment upon a loss.

---

[54] Paul Starr, "The Social Transformation of American Medicine." Basic Books, New York, 1982, p. 296
[55] HIAA (Health Insurance Association of America), Source Book of Health Insurance Data, 1990, 23.

Myth Busters

Because of its many regulatory advantages, Blue Cross quickly dominated the market for hospital financing, so other insurers learned how to replicate its third-party payment model, by using "assignment of benefits" and "participating provider" networks.

So, what difference does any of this make? It is enormous, especially in accountability and transparency

In a two-party contract there is direct accountability. I pay you for a service. I know exactly what I paid you and what you are supposed to do for the money. If you don't deliver the service or do a poor job I can sue you, or yell at you, or punch you in the nose. It is between you and me, and you do not want to make me angry.

In a three-party payment system there is no accountability. I go to the doctor and he does what he wants and somebody pays him. I don't know what he was paid or whether he did what he was supposed to do. But, importantly, the payer doesn't know, either! The payer may know what they paid, but they don't know what transpired between the doctor and me. The doctor doesn't know what my arrangement is with the insurer, either. He may not even know if what I want is a covered service or not.

Nobody knows anything. And so we spend way too much time trying to figure out what we don't know. The insurance company is very interested in what transpired, so they spend a lot of time getting the doctor to fill out forms and getting the patient to complete surveys. The doctor hires clerks to try to find out what is covered and for how much.

And I am simply baffled by the whole thing and annoyed about it all. I figure I can't trust any of these jokers because none of them cares about my well being in spite of all the money I (or my employer) shovel into their bank accounts. The doctor isn't working for me, he is working for the insurance company.

There is no way this arrangement can ever be made to work well.

Yet our system is fundamentally based on it. It was even adopted as the model for Medicare in 1965 with Part A covering hospital in-patient services like Blue Cross, and Part B covering physician office and outpatient care like Blue Shield. In fact, it has become so fundamental that most people cannot imagine any other way of doing it. And that is where the conversation usually stops.

Myth Busters #22: The Truth about the Individual Market, Part One

The individual market for health insurance has been long disparaged for being too expensive and too restrictive. The criticisms about health insurance are usually based on what the individual market is doing.

The promise by supporters of the Affordable Care Act, that people will no longer be turned down for coverage is an example. This was already illegal in all but the individual market. Even there, denials are a miniscule issue. According to a **recent report** by Milliman,[56] based on new reporting by carriers required by the National Association of Insurance Commissioners (NAIC), before the ACA there were only 10,300,000 people covered by individual health insurance – three percent of the population of the United States. And denials would happen only at the time of application for coverage, not after someone is already covered. The trade group America's Health Insurance Plans (AHIP) reported [57] that 87% of all applicants for individual coverage were accepted. Out of 1,763,000 applicants who were medically underwritten in 2008, AHIP reports that 223,000 were denied coverage. This is less than one tenth of one percent of the country's population.

The other criticism of the individual market is that it was too expensive. Milliman's analysis of the NAIC reports found that was simply not true. In fact, the premium per member per month for

---

[56] 2010 Commercial   Health Insurance Market: New Financial and Enrollment Data Available from the Supplemental Exhibit, Milliman, October, 2011. http://us.milliman.com/uploadedFiles/insight/health-published/health-insurance-market-10-31-11.pdf
[57] Individual Health Insurance, 2009, AHIP. https://kaiserhealthnews.files.wordpress.com/2013/02/2009individualmarketsurveyfinalreport.pdf

individual (non-group) coverage was $211.67, while the small group premium was $333.25 and large group was $333.74.

Milliman also found that the individual and small group markets had similar administrative costs on a per member/per month basis ($40.49 and $43.82, respectively), but both were higher than large group ($31.29), mostly due to "distribution costs" (marketing.) But because premiums were lower for individual coverage, similar expenses resulted in higher percentage of premiums. Thus, the individual market had a lower "loss ratio" (the percentage of premiums paid out in claims) of 80.9%) than small group (83.7%) or large group (89.3%).

What about market domination? Milliman found there were three states where a single carrier had 90% or more of market share in the large group market, two states for the small group market, and not a single state in the individual market. The number of states where a single carrier had 60% or more was 21 for large group, 17 for small group, and 15 for individual.

So what's going on here? The individual market was somewhat more competitive, had similar administrative costs, and considerably lower premiums than the small group and large group markets. Yet it is widely disparaged. Why?

The biggest reason is denials of coverage for new applicants. Only seven states required companies in the individual market to accept all applicants (guaranteed issue), but 33 of the remaining states had a high-risk pool that enrolled people who were denied, and for the rest, Miliman reports:

> "... the state may designate an insurer of last resort, have a specified product that is issued on a guaranteed basis, or require that each market participant insure a quota of high-risk individuals."

Now, it may be that these risk pools were underfunded and too restrictive, but the insurers can hardly be blamed for that. That is the responsibility of state legislatures. And it hardly seems rational to turn the entire health care system on its head to solve a problem that affects much fewer that one-tenth of one percent of the population.

The other problem, of course, was that benefits in the individual market were less generous than in the group market. These plans very often didn't cover prescription drugs or maternity, or required a separate rider for these benefits. But if the market wanted to buy coverage for these benefits, it is certain the insurers would be happy to sell them. But, when people buy their own coverage they tend to be more cautious in getting value for their money, and don't load up on things they don't think they will need. (See Chapter 15 on adverse selection)

The biggest problem in the individual market is that it wasn't subsidized, and we'll get into that in the next chapter.

Greg Scandlen

Myth Busters #23: The Truth about the Individual Market, Part Two

So, what was the problem with the individual market? As explained in the previous chapter, premiums were lower, administrative costs were similar, there was somewhat more competition, and most applicants who were rejected could find coverage in a risk pool, or would be able to if the pools had more financial support. Why does it continue to be the ugly stepchild of the health care system?

The answer is simple: it wasn't subsidized.

Every other form of insurance coverage gets massive subsidies. Obviously Medicare and Medicaid, being government programs, get most of their funding from taxpayers. Government spending on Medicare was **$555 billion** [58] in 2011 and **$387 billion** on Medicaid in 2009[59]. Employer-sponsored health insurance is also subsidized — to the tune of **over $300 billion a year,** according to the Congressional Research Service (CRS).[60] This is because the value of coverage provided by the employer is "excluded" from employees' income. Unlike wages, employees escape both income taxes and payroll taxes on this benefit. Prisoners, veterans, American Indians, all get subsidized health care. Even the uninsured are subsidized. The Kaiser Family Foundation found that, while the uninsured paid $30 billion for their own care in

[58] "The Facts on Medicare Sending and Financing," Kaiser Family Foundation, July 25, 2015. http://kff.org/medicare/fact-sheet/medicare-spending-and-financing-fact-sheet/
[59] "Medicaid Spending Growth over the Last Decade and the Great Recession, 2000-2009" Kaiser Family Foundation, February 1, 2011. http://kff.org/health-reform/report/medicaid-spending-growth-over-the-last-decade/
[60] Bob Lyke, "The Tax Exclusion for Employer-Provided Health Insurance: Policy Issues Regarding the Repeal Debate," Congressional Research Service, November 21, 2008. http://www.allhealth.org/briefingmaterials/rl34767-1359.pdf

2008, they incurred another **$56 billion in costs**, three-quarters of which was compensated for by government. [61]

Only people who buy their own coverage in the individual market get no tax break whatsoever. Actually, even that isn't quite true. In recent years the self-employed have been allowed to take a deduction of their health insurance premiums from their income, provided they make at least enough self-employment income to cover the expense. I haven't been able to track down the value of this tax break, but because they don't get to avoid the payroll tax the subsidy for the self-employed is still less generous than the complete exclusion from income of employer-sponsored coverage.

So who is left? Only those people who do not get coverage on the job, who are not self-employed, and who buy individual health insurance. These are the only people in America whose health insurance is not subsidized by the government.

Who are these unfortunates? They tend to be people of lower incomes. They may be unemployed or working only part time. They may be early retirees. If they are working, they are likely to be in low-paid jobs like retail clerks in small grocery stores, gardeners, busboys in restaurants, and the like.

Somehow the government has never seen fit to extend to these folks the kind of health insurance support the rest of us take for granted. Say what you will about ObamaCare, but for the first time in history it provided some "premium support" to this segment of the population.

Unfortunately, ObamaCare leaps over many less drastic steps that might have solved the problem without the wrenching contortions imposed by this law. We might have, for example, improved the individual market without a mandate.

---

[61] "New Study Examines the Current Spending on Health Care for the Uninsured and Projects the Cost of Additional Medical Care if the Population Were Insured," Kaiser Family Foundation, August 1, 2008. http://kff.org/health-reform/report/new-study-examines-the-current-spending-on/

Myth Busters

This might have been done simply by extending the same sort of subsidy to people who buy their own coverage as we give to those with employer-based coverage. Or, because the tax treatment of employer-based coverage is extremely regressive (higher-income people get more benefit than those with lower incomes), we might have reformed the whole thing to extend the same dollar amount to all who purchase health insurance, as John McCain proposed during the 2008 election. [62]

But let's assume for a minute that all private health insurance is treated the same way for tax purposes, whatever that treatment might be. What would happen then?

For most people nothing would change. Employers who find value in providing coverage would continue to do so. These might include companies in very competitive labor markets, or companies that are quite large and able to effectively pool their own risks, or companies with strong commitments to improving the health of their workforce through wellness programs and the like.

But, many other employers do not benefit from providing coverage. They may not have expertise on staff, or they might have high turnover, or be in relatively low-wage industries where cash wages are more attractive than insurance benefits. These companies could stop providing health insurance (many already have) and contribute to the cost of coverage for their employees instead.

The employees would no longer be disadvantaged by the tax code because the same tax benefit would be available whether they secured their own coverage or got it from the employer. This would be particularly beneficial for two-income families. They would be able to merge the resources of two employers into a single program for the entire family.

---

[62] John Goodman, "Is There a Republican Alternative to ObamaCare?" April 2, 2012. http://healthblog.ncpa.org/is-there-a-republican-alternative-to-obamacare/

But the greatest benefit would accrue to people who currently struggle to maintain their individual coverage. They may be only marginally attached to the workforce or work in jobs where the employer has no interest or few resources to finance health care. They might also be retired or physically unable to work. In all of these cases there would be tax support available that wasn't there before.

How would the insurance industry respond?

This is where our scenario gets really interesting. Let's assume that one-third of the current employer market switches to individual health insurance, in many cases with a contribution from the employer along with a tax credit from the government.

That would mean 50 million new customers in the individual market. Most of these people would be well-subsidized and relatively healthy since they are at least able to work. Would that be an attractive market? You betcha it would!

Suddenly the individual market would not be confined to the handful of people who simply cannot qualify for employer-sponsored coverage — people with sketchy work and health histories and dubious finances. Suddenly there would be a very large number of potential customers who are gainfully employed and financially secure. The insurance industry would be eager to enroll them.

The industry would immediately take several steps to gain a share of this attractive market;

- It would simplify the enrollment process to avoid alienating prospective customers.
- It would design benefit programs to be more appealing to specific market segments.
- It would start advertising directly to consumers, much as the auto insurance industry does today.
- New and innovative competitors would enter the market.

Myth Busters

- It would relax underwriting restrictions because the cost of underwriting would not be justified by the risk profile of the pool of applicants.

The last point needs to be explained a bit. As we've said, the current pool of applicants for coverage is very small and tends to be financially insecure and often in poor health. Carriers are cautious with this population because a handful of expensive people can have a large effect on the small enrollment base and the proportion of high risks is greater than in the general population. It is worth the expense of medical screening to protect the enrolled population from the cost of a few high-cost cases.

Once the pool of applicants is more like the general population it is no longer worth the cost of screening 100% of the applicants to keep out the very small number of high risks. Medical screening also tends to alienate the good risks the company would like to attract.

There might still be a very simplified health statement required, but this might be confined to a checklist of ten (or so) questions looking for active cases of cancer or heart disease. These applicants would be referred to the high-risk pool. Every voluntary insurance market has some form of high-risk pool, usually referred to as a "residual market."

This simple change in tax policy would lead to a much more competitive and innovative insurance market, and would make health insurance coverage far more affordable to people not benefitting from employer-sponsored care.

It could lead to expanded insurance coverage as ObamaCare tried to do, but with far fewer regulations, mandates, and complexity, and much lower system-wide costs.

Myth Busters #24: The "Burden" of High Deductibles

The folks at Harvard really, really hate cost sharing (i.e., deductibles, coinsurance and co-pays) in health care. They are much less concerned about high premiums or taxes. At least that is the conclusion one might draw from an article in **Health Affairs.**[63]

The authors examined the fate of 393 families enrolled in high-deductible plans through Massachusetts' Commonwealth Connector (a precursor of ObamaCare's exchanges). The families were well off enough to be unsubsidized and enrolled in a Harvard Pilgrim health plan. These were compared to similar families in plans with no deductible. They were looking for –

> "...respondents' reports of any financial burden, higher-than-expected out-of-pocket costs, or discussions of costs with doctors. To measure financial burden, we asked enrollees whether, in the prior twelve months in the Connector plan, they or a family member had had problems paying or had been unable to pay medical bills; had had to set up a payment plan with a hospital or doctor's office; or had had trouble paying for other basic needs such as food, heat, and rent because of medical costs. An affirmative answer to any of these three questions was considered an indication of financial burden."

So right off the bat, the authors are judging that any discussion of costs with a doctor is a bad thing, and any "payment plan" is a "burden." You can see where this is going. One might think that

---

[63] Alison A. Galbraith, et. al., "Some Families Who Purchased Health Coverage Through The Massachusetts Connector Wound Up With High Financial Burdens," Health Affairs.
http://content.healthaffairs.org/content/early/2013/04/15/hlthaff.2012.0864

discussing costs with a doctor would be a good thing, but not to the folks at Harvard. And, by golly, using these criteria the researchers found that lots of folks are "burdened." They write –

> "Among families in such plans, those with lower incomes, worse health, and more children were at greater risk for financial burden and higher-than-expected out-of-pocket costs. Families in high-deductible plans were also more likely to have higher-than-expected costs than were families in plans with no deductible."

The authors are remarkably unconcerned about what it would have cost these unsubsidized families to avoid such burdens. But they include a table that provides a hint — if you compare the difference in annual premium to the annual deductible, as I do below. Gold plans have zero deductibles.

	Bronze Plan Premium	Gold Plan Premium	Difference	Maximum Bronze Deductible
Individual	2,700	4,680	1,980	1,750
Family	9,526	16,716	7,190	3,500

So families with "high deductibles" of $3,500 or less are "burdened" even though they would have to pay $7,190 in higher premiums to avoid the deductible. Keep in mind that the premium is lost money. The family would have to pay that every year no matter how little health care they consume. The deductible may not be paid at all in a given year, or a family may have to pay only a portion of it.

But our friends at Harvard have no trouble burdening families with very high premiums (or taxes) provided they don't have to pay for any of the health care they actually consume or (heaven forbid) have a discussion with the doctor about the cost of the care he or she is providing.

Interestingly, these same people seem unconcerned about the deductibles that are commonplace under ObamaCare, where $6,000 or more has become almost standard. There has been very little handwringing or scholarly articles about the horrific burden the Affordable Care Act places on American families. Funny how that works.

Greg Scandlen

Myth Busters #25: Population Health

The idea of "Population Health" is a huge new trend that has arisen under the radar of almost the entire population. Nearly every medical school now has a Department of Population Health or a Center for Population Health. Thomas Jefferson University has an entire school devoted to the subject — **The Jefferson School of Population Health,** founded in 2008.[64]

The concept is kind of creepy, but it is getting even creepier. The Institute for Healthcare Improvement (IHI), Don Berwick's old outfit, announced a conference on "**Population Management**" to be held September 28 to October 1, 2014.[65] Enrollment cost $4,950 per person, so you know it was a very big deal.

One of the reasons it is hard to write about this is there is no settled definition of what it is. A **paper** written in 2003 by David Kindig and Greg Stoddard in the American Journal of Public Health took a stab at it.[66] They write –

> "Although the term "population health" has been much more commonly used in Canada than in the United States, a precise definition has not been agreed upon even in Canada, where the concept it denotes has gained some prominence."

---

[64] http://www.jefferson.edu/university/population-health.html
[65]
http://www.ihi.org/education/InPersonTraining/PopHealthMgmt/2014SeptPopMgmt/Pages/default.aspx?utm_campaign=Pop%20Management%20Sept&utm_medium=google%20adwords&utm_source=ppc&
[66] David Kindig and Dave Stoddard, "What is Population Health?" American Journal of Public Health, March, 2003.
https://www.ncbi.nlm.nih.gov/pmc/articles/PMC1447747/

They proceeded to define it as "the health outcomes of a group of individuals, including the distribution of such outcomes within the group." They go on to explain –

> "We support the idea that a hallmark of *the field of population health* is significant attention to the multiple determinants of such health outcomes, however measured. These determinants include medical care, public health interventions, aspects of the social environment (income, education, employment, social support, culture) and of the physical environment (urban design, clean air and water), genetics, and individual behavior."

In other words: Everything under the sun.

Such an all-inclusive definition is not very helpful, so people keep trying. Ten years later Michael Stoto gave it a shot in a **paper** published by Academy Health, "Population Health in the Affordable Care Act Era."[67] This paper spends half its space explaining some of the different definitions currently in use. The balance of the paper is suggesting to researchers how they can tailor their projects to take advantage of funding opportunities presented by ObamaCare.

The same year the Robert Wood Johnson Foundation published a **series of blogs** by Nicholas Stine and Dave Chockshi on Population Health [68] that started with one attempt to define it. They interviewed 17 "leaders" of the population health movement and found that each one has a different definition.

Now this is very peculiar. Vast resources are being invested into something that cannot be defined. What's going on here?

It is chilling. First, it seems to be a raw power grab. The Kindig/Stoddard definition would place virtually every human

---

[67] http://www.academyhealth.org/publications/2013-02/population-health-affordable-care-act-era

[68] http://www.rwjf.org/en/culture-of-health/2013/01/defining_population.html

activity under the management of "population health" experts —
food, education, the arts, architecture, even "individual behavior"
— all must bend to the demands of the new "population health"
system. Add in Don Berwick's concept of "population
management" and we get a tiny elite anointed to manage the
behavior of the entire population, all in the name of improving
their health whether they want it or not.

Clearly these people are bored with the idea of treating one patient
at a time. That is far too messy, and actual people are not very
pleasant to deal with. It is much more grandiose and ego enhancing
to "treat" and control the activities of the *ENTIRE
POPULATION!* This impulse is identical to that of Progressives
who are in love with "the people," but don't much care for actual
persons.

Even more chilling is the realization that in dealing with the health
of a "population," the needs of any individual are simply
unimportant. Things become measured by averages. The average
result will improve if we eliminate the outliers who bring down the
average. This is sometimes known as thinning the herd. If we
could rid ourselves of those people with serious disease, we would
have a much healthier population, on average.

This calculation becomes even more compelling when costs are
considered, as Kindig and Stoddard write –

> "In our view, a population health perspective also requires
> attention to the resource allocation issues involved in
> linking determinants to outcomes. Part of the study of
> population health involves the estimation of the cross-
> sectoral cost-effectiveness of different types and
> combinations of investments for producing health."

This is how the sickest people get left behind. Spend a little bit of
money on "preventive care" to improve the health of the majority
by a small margin, but forget about expensive organ transplants.

The result is an improvement in the health of the population at very low cost.

The mathematics of population health drive these conclusions. And the current adoration of Zeke Emanuel and Peter Singer suggests that this is exactly what lies ahead as long as we keep empowering the elite rather than the people. See, for instance, my article in The Federalist on Emanuel's proposal that people reaching age 75 have a duty to die to save the system money. [69]

[69] Greg Scandlen, "Zeke Emanuel Wants You to Die at 75," The Federalist, September 23, 2014. http://thefederalist.com/2014/09/23/zeke-emanuel-wants-you-to-die-at-75/

Myth Busters #26: Dying in the Hospital

When we last looked at the Dartmouth Health Atlas it was worrying about hysterectomies in Lewiston, Maine (see chapter 2). In the intervening years it cranked out dozens of studies purporting to show how terrible American health care is. They typically base their findings on Medicare claims data and then pretend what happens with Medicare can be extrapolated to the entire population. It also routinely ignores patient demands and resources, in the belief that everything that happens in health care is because of greedy doctors and hospitals (remember Roemer's Law?)

For example, a few years ago it come out with another one of its national breakdowns of Medicare claims, showing a wide variation between areas. This one is focused on end-of-life care for people with chronic illnesses. [70]

The authors, David Goodman, Amos Esty, Elliott Fisher, and Chiang-Hua Chang do their usual job of putting vast amounts of data into very colorful maps, which add up to absolutely no understanding of what is going on.

They find, for instance, that:

> Widespread regional variation persists in measures of end-of-life care. In 2007, the percentage of deaths in hospital varied by a factor of almost four across hospital referral regions, and the average number of hospice days per patient in the last six months of life varied by a factor of more than six.

---

[70] David Goodman, et.al., "Trends and Variations in End of Life Care for Medicare Beneficiaries with Severe Chronic Illness, April 12, 2011 http://www.dartmouthatlas.org/downloads/reports/EOL_Trend_Report_0411.pdf

Greg Scandlen

More specifically, the authors found for in-hospital deaths:

> In 2007, the highest rates of death in hospital were in
> regions in and around New York City, including Manhattan
> (45.8%), East Long Island (41.9%) and the Bronx (39.9%).
> Chronically ill Medicare beneficiaries in Manhattan were
> far more likely to die in a hospital than patients in Minot,
> North Dakota, where only 12.0% of patients died in a
> hospital. Fort Lauderdale, Florida (19.0%) and Portland,
> Oregon (19.6%) were also among the regions with the
> lowest rates.

And for lengths of hospital stays in the last six months of life, they
found:

> In 2007, patients in Manhattan spent, on average, 20.6 days
> in the hospital during their last six months of life, almost
> four times more than patients in Ogden, Utah, where the
> average was 5.2 days. Other regions in New York and
> regions in New Jersey also had among the highest rates,
> including East Long Island (18.9) and the Bronx (18.1) in
> New York, and Newark (17.7), New Brunswick (17.5),
> Hackensack (17.2), Paterson (17.0) and Ridgewood (16.8)
> in New Jersey. Regions with the lowest average number of
> hospital days were found largely in the West and Midwest,
> including, in addition to Ogden, Salt Lake City (6.2),
> Portland, Oregon (7.2) and Spokane, Washington (7.4).

Now the authors claim that they have accounted for variations in
populations and adjusted for that:

> Although it is possible that some of the differences across
> hospitals may be explained by differences in patients'
> preferences for care, studies show that regional variation in
> patient preferences overall explains very little of the
> variation in the intensity of end-of-life care. Differences in
> patient populations themselves also explain some of the

variation in care. But by examining patients close to the end of life who are similarly ill with severe chronic diseases, and by adjusting for differences in age, sex, race and illness—as the data in this report have been adjusted— it is possible to account for most of the variation in patient populations, leaving variation caused by other factors, such as the availability of medical resources and the practice styles of health systems and clinicians. As this report shows, the remaining variation is substantial, both in the use of medical care and in trends in end-of-life care.

So the authors smugly assume that by adjusting for age, sex, race, and illness, they have eliminated any population differences that might contribute to different courses of treatment.

Golly, might there be anything else that distinguishes people in New York City from people in Ogden, Utah or Minot, North Dakota that might cause one population to be treated differently at the end of their lives? Let's put on our thinking caps and noodle on this really, really hard.

Just maybe some people have different family structures and living conditions that enable them to stay at home during their last days, and just maybe these conditions are more favorable in Ogden and Minot than in New York. Conditions such as –

- Owning their own homes.
- Having intact families around, including adult children.
- Being strongly religious, especially Mormon in Ogden.
- Living in the same community all their lives.
- Residing in one or two story homes, rather than walk-up apartments.
- Having well-established networks of friends and civic associations.
- Enjoying a low rate of crime.

The Dartmouth researchers saw no need to ask about any of these conditions. They were content with things like race and gender. But like most health policy researchers, these folks view patients as slabs of flesh to be pushed around rather than as fully-realized adult human beings.

It is true they had the patients fill out a "patient preferences" questionnaire, but just because someone may "prefer" to die at home doesn't mean they are practicably able to do so.
Now this is no obscure research project with little effect on real-world policy. Indeed, one of the authors, Elliot Fisher, is the primary force behind the Obama administration's devotion to Accountable Care Organizations. If the thinking going in to ACOs is as shallow as the thinking in this paper, we can be assured that the needs of actual real-life patients will be well down the list of priorities.

One final thought: If you download the study and look at the pretty maps, you will notice an almost perfect correlation between the areas where people most often die in the hospital and the areas where people are most likely to vote for Democrats. So here is another variable that stands out – the political orientation of the population. Is it possible that Democratic patients have an entitlement mentality that demands they be taken care of, while Republican patients are more self-reliant? Inquiring minds want to know.

Myth Busters #27: Value Based Payments

In Information Week, David Carr **writes** about some of the current trends in health care, and especially about "value based payments." [71] He writes –

> "'Value based' is a catch-all label for Accountable Care Organizations (ACOs) and other ways of restructuring healthcare around payment for value delivered, as measured by metrics of healthcare quality or the aggregate health of a population rather than by the volume of visits, procedures, or hospital stays a healthcare organization records. In other words, it's a highly data-driven vision of healthcare reform, intended to improve quality and efficiency while reducing costs."

He reports on a **study** by Availity [72] that says while 75% of providers currently participate in some form of "value-based payment model…fewer than 30% believe these schemes offer a good level of reward for the risk." Generally, both physicians and hospitals are concerned about the additional administrative burden and expense needed to justify payment.

This growth in administrative costs is no small thing. As the chart below shows there has been an enormous increase of administrators in the health care system, especially since managed care became prominent in the mid-1980s. It could be argued that all of the increase in health care costs can be attributed to this

---

[71] David F. Carr, "Physicians, Hospitals Size Up Value-Based Healthcare," InformationWeek, May 29, 2014.
http://www.informationweek.com/healthcare/policy-and-regulation/physicians-hospitals-size-up-value-based-healthcare/d/d-id/1269249
[72] "Study Reveals Provider Concerns With Value-based Payment Models," Availity, https://www.availity.com/about-us/news-center/study-reveals-provider-concerns-value-based-payment-models

growth – with no contribution to patient care. You will note that we also presented this chart in Chapter 6 about Business Coalitions in the mid 1980s. Now we see the consequences of the growth in bureaucracy.

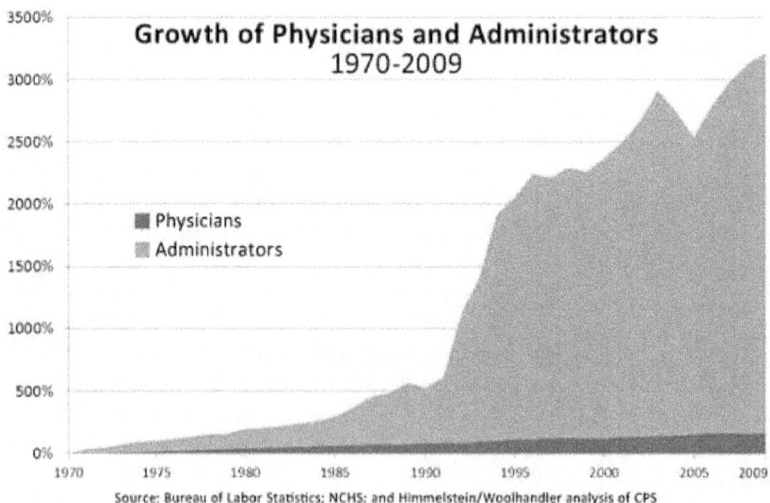

Growth of Physicians and Administrators 1970-2009

Source: Bureau of Labor Statistics; NCHS; and Himmelstein/Woolhandler analysis of CPS

That concern is certainly borne out by an **article** titled "What is Value in Health Care?" from the New England Journal of Medicine published in 2010 and written by Michael Porter of the Harvard Business School.[73]

Porter is extremely well regarded, so what he writes must be taken seriously. But there is something about health care that makes even sensible people lose their grip. Porter starts off with –

> "In any field, improving performance and accountability depends on having a shared goal that unites the interests and activities of all stakeholders."

That sounds very insightful and meaningful, but is it remotely true? I can't think of a single instance of its being true.

---

[73] http://www.nejm.org/doi/pdf/10.1056/NEJMp1011024

Myth Busters

Before Bill Gates and Steve Jobs, did the computer industry have a "shared goal that united the activities of all stakeholders?" What would that "shared goal" have been? Did the goal change when Microsoft and Apple came along? It would seem that the goal of these two companies was to eat IBM's lunch. I doubt IBM shared that goal.

Ditto with every significant innovation, ever. The "shared goal" of existing stakeholders is to divvy up the market and keep out competitors. Is that really how performance and accountability are improved? The "shared goal" of new competitors is to get rid of the old "stakeholders" and persuade consumers that there are new and better ways to fulfill their needs.

Porter actually knows this. In 2008 the Harvard Business Review published an **update** of Porter's "Five Forces" analysis of competitive dynamics [74] that included his famous graphic –

The Five Forces That Shape Industry Competition

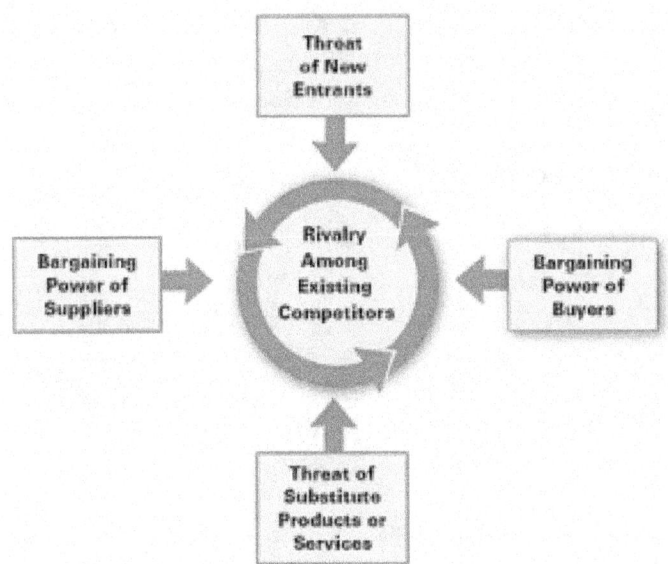

---

[74] https://hbr.org/2008/01/the-five-competitive-forces-that-shape-strategy

Where is the "shared goal that unites the interests and activities of all stakeholders" in this?

Porter's NEJM article goes on with some useful suggestions but an awful lot of platitudes. For instance, he says that health care should be based on value to the patient, "value" being defined as "outcomes relative to costs." Then he writes –

> "Outcomes, the numerator of the value equation, are inherently condition-specific and multidimensional. For any medical condition, no single outcome captures the results of care."

But a "numerator" is by definition a number. How can we develop a single number to represent outcomes when they are so "multidimensional" and "condition specific?"

In fact, I would argue that the whole idea that "value to the patient" can be defined objectively is misguided. Even with precisely the same cost and the same medical outcome, the "value" of a service will be different for every patient. Dick Cheney seemed to be very happy with his heart transplant and thrilled to extend his life by several more years. Someone else might think that the ordeal of the surgery and medical attention isn't worth it. Or they might think that their life is pretty crappy and not worth extending.

This doesn't apply just to health care. The value of a new Mercedes is different for you and me. You might think having such a car is proof to the world that you have arrived: it shows how successful and prosperous you are. I might be embarrassed by the conspicuous consumption and prefer something more modest. I might prefer to spend the money on charitable contributions. The difference is entirely subjective.

The balance of Porter's article illustrates how futile his quest is. Some quotes –

- "Because care activities are interdependent, value for patients is often revealed only over time and is manifested in longer-term outcomes such as sustainable recovery, need for ongoing interventions, or occurrences of treatment-induced illnesses

- "For patients with multiple medical conditions, value should be measured for each condition, with the presence of the other conditions used for risk adjustment.
- "The concept of quality has itself become a source of confusion.
- "No organization I know of systematically measures the entire outcome hierarchy for the medical conditions for which it provides services
- "Current cost-measurement approaches have also obscured value in health care and led to cost- containment efforts that are incremental, ineffective, and some-times even counterproductive."

Whew! What a great number of windmills for this Don Quixote to attack!

Greg Scandlen

Myth Busters #28: The Health Information Technology (HIT) Panacea

Over a decade ago the media was excited that Hillary Clinton and Newt Gingrich had formed an alliance about reforming health care. In 2005 Dana Milbank wrote in the **Washington Post** [75] about a joint appearance in gushing terms –

> "Clinton, asked about electronic medical records, deferred, again, to her friend. 'Newt has a very dramatic way of saying this,' she said, 'which is 'Paper kills.'" Gingrich sent the praise right back at her, hailing Clinton's legislation on medical records as a 'major breakthrough' in Congress. 'This is absolutely the case that Hillary is making,' he said."

Of course, they were not alone. President Bush had already embraced the idea in his **State of the Union speech to Congress.**[76]

Later, President Obama built the HITECH Act into his 2009 stimulus package and appropriated some $20 billion to make it happen. All promised to get everyone's complete medical records in digital form by 2014.

Man, this is going to be GREAT! A model of modern efficiency! Bipartisan support! Interoperable! WOWSA!

Now, of course there were the usual naysayers and Gloomy Gusses. I was one of them in this research and commentary I

---

[75] Dana Milbank, "The Reformer and the Gadfly Agree on Health Care," Washington Poat, July 22, 2005. http://www.washingtonpost.com/wp-dyn/content/article/2005/07/21/AR2005072102272.html
[76] Declan McCullagh, "Bush Calls for Electronic Medical Records," C/NET, February 3, 2005. https://www.cnet.com/news/bush-calls-for-computerized-medical-records/

wrote for the Heartland Institute.[77] Dr. Bruce Landes [78] was another. Dr. Scott Silverstein at Drexel University was also skeptical.[79] And Dr. Deborah Peele was very concerned about patient privacy in a digital era.[80]

Most of these concerns were not about whether digital technology is a good thing. Of course it is, or can be, a very good thing. But the track record of top-down, politically imposed solutions is abysmal. And when you add vast amounts of money to the mix, chaos is inevitable. Great Britain went through a similar, though more modest, exercise to upgrade the health information technology within the National Health Service and recently concluded that the whole thing was a failure, but only after spending some $12 billion on it.

But we skeptics were not able to overcome the hordes of advocates who were eager to get their hands on a bit of the $20 billion.

Now the results of all this are coming to the fore. The *Washington Post* recently ran an **op-ed piece by Dr. Dan Morhaim,** [81] who is also a Democrat member of Maryland's House of Delegates. (One of the refreshing things about bipartisan ideas is that the opposition can also be bipartisan.) He writes –

> "These systems tend to be fantastically complex. One doesn't have to be intimately familiar with, say, Hertz or Enterprise to rent a car online. But many electronic health record systems have pull-down screens listing each of the 68,000 possible diagnosis codes in the World Health

[77] Greg Scandlen, "R&C: Health Information Technology," Heartland Institute, February 20, 2009. https://www.heartland.org/publications-resources/publications/research--commentary-health-information-technology?source=policybot
[78] http://www.healthleadersmedia.com/technology/emr-wars-part-ii
[79] http://cci.drexel.edu/faculty/ssilverstein/cases/?loc=about
[80] http://patientprivacyrights.org/
[81] Dan Morhaim, "An Electronic Medical Records Mess," Washington Post, September 27, 2013. https://www.washingtonpost.com/opinions/americas-electronic-medical-records-mess/2013/09/27/651a81f0-2716-11e3-b75d-5b7f66349852_print.html

Organization's International Classification of Diseases and 87,000 possible procedure codes.

"Or consider what happens when I write a prescription: Every potential drug interaction or side effect listed generates a warning prompt. Inevitably, recognizing that the warnings are generally inapplicable and take time to sort out, clinicians start to bypass the alerts. Sooner or later, ignoring one will lead to serious complications."

Dr. Morhaim concludes –

"Perhaps the most pernicious side effect is the erosion of the provider-patient relationship. When I first began working with electronic health records, I caught myself staring at the computer screen instead of engaging patients, who rightly felt ignored. Like many colleagues, I've reverted to the practice of talking with the patient and taking notes with pen and paper. After the evaluation is over and the patient has left, I type in the data. This takes much more time, but it is the only way to complete a proper history and exam.

"The result is decreased productivity and frustrated providers — and a lack of meaningful data to manage patient care."

And *The American Journal of Emergency Medicine* published a study [82] finding that ER physicians are now spending 43% of their time on data entry and only 28% on direct patient care.

So we have spent well over $20 billion (that was the appropriation for the first year alone), and are left with a system that reduces productivity, fails to provide "meaningful data," and destroys the

---

[82] Susan London, "Physicians Spend More Time on EMRs Than With Patients in ED," Medscape, September 27, 2013.
http://www.medscape.com/viewarticle/811841

patient/physician relationship. From 2011 to 2012 there was a 21% reduction in the number of family physicians who had "meaningful use" of electronic medical records, according to the **American Association of Family Physicians.**[83] Yet the mandate to use this system continues.

[83] "EHR Meaningful Use Dropout Rate Soars in 2012," July 3, 2013. http://www.aafp.org/news/practice-professional-issues/20130703mudropoutrate.html

Myth Busters #29: Health Information Technology (HIT) Gets Worse

Our last chapter described some of the warning signs that HIT would not be the panacea proponents had promised. Information keeps rolling in that it is even worse than we imagined.

Articles from **the New York Times** [84] and the **RAND Corporation** [85] indicate that HIT has not lived up to expectations. Actually, it is quite a bit worse than that. The RAND piece is a sort of *mea culpa* for an earlier **RAND "study"** [86] that predicted $81 billion in annual savings if we adopted HIT. This RAND piece was the main rationale for spending over $20 billion on HIT, but rather than saving money, HIT seems to have cost more money because it made it easier to bill for more services, according to the Times. It may also be creating more errors and inefficiencies in medical practice.

None of this should have some as a surprise. It was widely predicted back when Congress was considering including HIT in the stimulus legislation. President Obama was quoted at the time as saying, "We will make the immediate investments necessary to ensure that within five years all of America's medical records are computerized." Mr. Obama may be forgiven his blind optimism, after all Newt Gingrich and Hillary Clinton had joined together to make similar promises.

---

[84] Reed Abelson and Julie Creswell, "In Second Look, Few Savings From Digital Health Records," New York Times, January 10, 2013. http://www.nytimes.com/2013/01/11/business/electronic-records-systems-have-not-reduced-health-costs-report-says.html?emc=tnt&tntemail0=y&_r=2&
[85] Arthur Kellerman and Spencer Jones, "What It Will Take To Achieve The As-Yet-Unfulfilled Promises Of Health Information Technology," Health Affairs, http://content.healthaffairs.org/content/32/1/63.abstract
[86] Richard Hillestad, et. al. "Health Information Technology: Can HIT Lower Costs and Improve Quality?" RAND Corporation. http://www.rand.org/pubs/research_briefs/RB9136.html

But the people who actually knew something about this and were not lusting after a piece of the $20 billion piñata universally said the opposite — that a top-down bureaucratic system would not work very well and might actually cost more money and result in worse care.

Jerome Groopman, MD and Pamela Hartzband, MD, both on the faculty of Harvard Medical School, wrote in the **Wall Street Journal** [87] that, "The basis for the president's proposal is a theoretical study published in 2005 by the RAND Corporation (but) in the four years since the report, considerable data have been obtained that undermine their claims." They call the proposal, "an elegant exercise in wishful thinking." They add that the RAND researchers deliberately avoided looking at any negative information, saying, "We choose to interpret reported evidence of negative or no effect of health information technology as likely being attributable to ineffective or not-yet-effective implementation."

And in the **Washington Post**, Stephan Soumerai and Sumit Majumdar wrote that Obama was making a "Bad Bet on Medical Records."[88] The first author was a professor at Harvard's Medical School and the second was at the University of Alberta's Medical School. They wrote that, "The benefits of health IT have been greatly exaggerated." Specifically, they said, "Large, randomized controlled studies — the "gold standard" of evidence — in this country and Britain have found that electronic records with computerized decision support did not result in a single improvement in any measure of quality of care for patients with chronic conditions including heart disease and asthma." And, they add, "Health IT has not been proven to save money."

---

[87] "Obama's $80 Billion Exaggeration," Wall Street Journal, March 12, 2009. https://www.wsj.com/articles/SB123681586452302125
[88] "A Bad $50 Billion Bet," Washington Post, March 17, 2009. http://www.washingtonpost.com/wp-dyn/content/article/2009/03/16/AR2009031602618.html

Myth Busters

In the real world, the UK's $12 billion effort to computerize medical records in the National Health Service was already falling apart, according to a **report** to Parliament. [89] This was followed up a few years later by a candid admission by the government that it had wasted all the money and was closing down the program.

Even more modest efforts by our own government had already failed. The Veterans Administration spent $167 million to simply computerize its appointments system. This effort had "all but collapsed, and senior executives are worried about the repercussions it could cause on the Hill and in the White House, according to an internal memo obtained by **NextGov** (a trade publication)." [90]

At the Department of Defense "top health officials lambasted the department's central electronic health record system that manages patient files for millions of active duty and retired service members, saying it frustrates doctors because it crashes as often as once a week and generates duplicate records," again, according to **NextGov**. [91] The article goes on to quote the Deputy Surgeon General of the Air Forces as saying the system was, "slow, unreliable and so cumbersome that clinicians spend 40 percent of their time inputting data into the system, which is time spent away from patients."

There was absolutely no evidence that this massive spending would succeed, and plenty that it would fail miserably. Now, even the editors of the **Washington Post** [92] came to agree the whole

---

[89] The National Programme for IT in the NHS: Progress since 2006 - Public Accounts Committee
https://www.publications.parliament.uk/pa/cm200809/cmselect/cmpubacc/153/15304.htm

[90] Bob Brewin, "VA System to Schedule Appointments on Verge of Collapse." NextGov, March 31,2009. http://www.nextgov.com/health/2009/03/officials-criticize-defenses-unreliable-health-record-system/43412/

[91] Bob Brewin, "Officials Criticize Defense's Unreliable Health Data System," NextGov, March 24, 2009. http://www.nextgov.com/health/2009/03/officials-criticize-defenses-unreliable-health-record-system/43412/

[92] "The Rush to Digitize Patient Records has no cut Costs," Washington Post editorial, January 14, 2013. https://www.washingtonpost.com/opinions/the-rush-

project was a fiasco — but only after we wasted $27 billion of taxpayer money.

Yet, those who are enriching themselves on the $27 billion are just happy as clams over the program. John Hoyt, the Executive Vice President of the Healthcare Information and Management Systems Society (HIMSS) was quoted in a recent issue of Healthcare Informatics as saying –

> "This data suggests that the HITECH portion of the 2009 stimulus law is achieving its intended result of encouraging increased implementation and meaningful use of electronic health records among hospitals." [93]

There, aren't you greatly reassured? By the way, the New York Times piece cited above reported that –

> "RAND's **2005 report** was paid for by a group of companies, including General Electric and Cerner Corporation, which have profited by developing and selling electronic records systems to hospitals and physician practices. Cerner's revenue has nearly tripled since the report was released, to a projected $3 billion in 2013, from $1 billion in 2005."

No doubt the companies that paid for the RAND study are also members of HIMSS. And General Electric certainly had what might be called a "special" relationship with President Obama.

---

to-digitize-patient-records-has-not-cut-costs/2013/01/14/09d90096-5c2d-11e2-beee-6e38f5215402_story.html?hpid=z3&utm_term=.5c39cb6f4ec9
[93] Gabriel Pema, "HIMSS Analytics: HITECH Achieving its Intended Result" Healthcare Informatics, January 17, 2013. http://www.healthcare-informatics.com/news-item/himss-analytics-hitech-achieving-its-intended-result?page=4

Myth Busters #30: The Illusion of Mandatory Coverage

Health reform has long been tainted by the bumper sticker slogan of "universal health insurance" in the minds of most reformers. If health reform did not include universality it was not worth pursuing, in their view.

How can we make sure it is universal? Simple. Pass a law mandating that everyone must buy it or be punished! Problem solved. No sweat.

Alas. Things are never that simple.

In an enormous, dynamic, and fluid nation like ours it is impossible to get "everyone" to do anything. It doesn't matter the size of the penalty. It doesn't matter how easy compliance might be. There is always a contingent of the population that won't do it. In 2007, a cautionary study was published in Health Affairs laying out what was known about mandates at the time. [94] It found that the rate of compliance for all kinds of mandatory behavior was not much different than the rate of purchasing health insurance on a voluntary basis:

- Paying child support is mandatory, but only 30 percent of mothers receive it
- States with mandatory childhood immunizations had a compliance rate of 85 percent.
- Paying individual income taxes is mandatory, but only 84.5 percent comply.
- Paying minimum wage is mandatory but compliance runs between 65 -75 percent.

---

[94] Sherry Glied, et. al. "Consider it Done? The Likely Efficacy of Mandates for Health Insurance," Health Affairs, 2007.
http://content.healthaffairs.org/content/26/6/1612.abstract

- Even with auto insurance, the states without a mandate had a lower rate of uninsured motorists that the ones with a mandate.
- The one exception was helmet laws for motorcycle riders. Here compliance was near-universal, but the bikers resented it so much that they got the laws repealed in over half the states.

The case of auto insurance is especially enlightening. According to 2004 numbers, all but three states had enacted mandatory auto insurance, sometimes with pretty severe penalties for noncompliance – In Kentucky an uninsured motorist can be fined $1,000 and 6 months in jail; Wyoming also has a 6 month jail term and a $750 fine; In Louisiana, the driver's car can be impounded for failure to insure. Yet the rate of noncompliance was 12 percent in Kentucky, 11 percent in Wyoming and 10 percent in Louisiana. In seventeen states the rate of non-insurance for auto, which was mandated, was higher than the rate of non-insurance for health, which was not. [95]

The persistence of non-insurance for health care is one of the most steady "trends" you will ever find in human behavior. Let's look again at the graph we featured in Chapter 9. The data below is from a report on insurance coverage by the Employee Benefit Research Institute (EBRI). [96] It is based on Census Bureau numbers from 1994 through 2012. Every year about 84% of the non-elderly population has health insurance coverage and 16% does not. The number wobbles a little bit during recessions, but not by much. It doesn't matter how many new programs are enacted, how many new incentives are offered, or how much the cost of coverage goes up, the percentages stay the same.

---

[95] Greg Scandlen, "Will Mandatory Health Insurance Work?" National Center for Policy Analysis, September 6, 2006. http://www.ncpa.org/pub/ba569
[96] "Sources of Health Insurance and Characteristics of the Uninsured: Analysis of the March 2013 Current Population Survey," EBRI, September, 2013, https://www.ebri.org/publications/ib/index.cfm?fa=ibDisp&content_id=5272

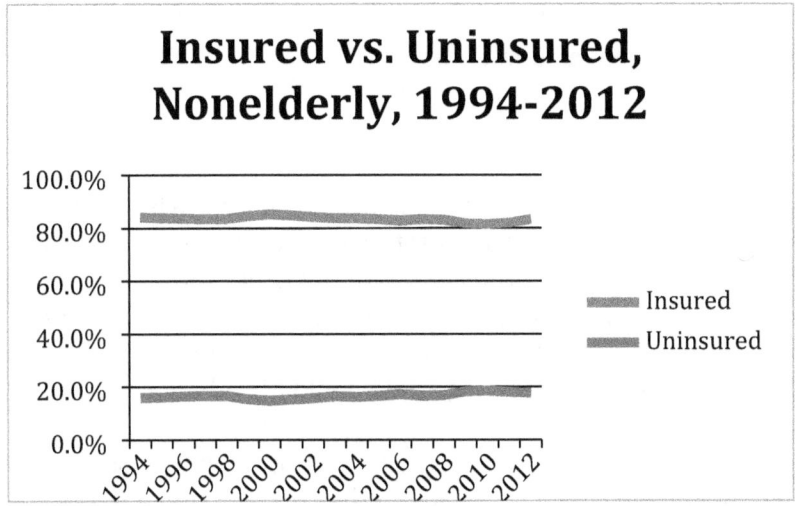

Insured vs. Uninsured, Nonelderly, 1994-2012

In fact, there is a good-sized portion of the population that is incapable of managing health insurance of any kind. They might be illiterate or mentally ill or drug addicted or in the underground economy or simply have poor impulse control. They can't read a contract, can't keep an appointment to see a doctor, and can't follow prescribed treatment programs.

These folks don't need insurance, they need a source of health care services. They will wait till they feel poorly and roll down to the emergency room like they always have because that is where the doctors are. In Massachusetts the use of emergency department services went up, not down, after the mandate went into effect there.

Even a free public insurance program like Medicaid isn't the answer. Some one-third of the uninsured were already eligible for Medicaid before Obamacare was enacted, but simply hadn't enrolled. A study a few years ago in the journal Health Affairs found that one-third of all children eligible for Medicaid or S-CHIP *had been enrolled in the program in the previous year* but their parents didn't bother re-enrolling them.[97] It wasn't that they didn't know about it or they didn't know how to enroll. They simply weren't motivated to do it.

What About "Free Riders?"

Obviously these people will continue to receive care whether they are insured or not, so the primary rationale for mandatory coverage – solving the "free rider" problem – will not be solved. Yes, it may be reduced, but it would be reduced anyway if the subsidies were available without a mandate. More people would buy insurance on a voluntary basis because more people could afford it.

And uncompensated care ("free riding") is not an enormous problem in any event. Most serious studies place it at about 3% of total health care costs. This is lower than the losses to retailers from shoplifting and employee theft (see Chapter 8). It is just a cost of doing business in a free society.

Further, while uncompensated care may raise costs for the insured, those costs do not disappear with a mandate. They are simply transferred over to the tax system and used to subsidize coverage rather than subsidizing the care itself.

Indeed, if we consider all of the federal subsidies paid out to various people, the costs to taxpayers makes the cost of uncompensated care seem trivial. The American Hospital Association estimates that uncompensated care cost hospitals $41 billion in 2011, while the Urban Institute estimated the exclusion from taxes of employer-sponsored health insurance alone cost the federal government $268 billion in foregone revenues. Throw in subsidies provided for Medicare, Medicaid, and hundreds of other federal programs, the money you pay to subsidize other people through your taxes are massive compared to the extra premiums you might pay for uncompensated care.

---

[97] Benjamin D. Sommers, "Why Millions Of Children Eligible For Medicaid And SCHIP Are Uninsured: Poor Retention Versus Poor Take-Up," Health Affairs. http://content.healthaffairs.org/content/26/5/w560.short

Myth Busters

What should be done?

The goal of making health insurance coverage more affordable and more accessible is a good one, even if it will never be universal. So what should be done?

First, we should look at the uninsured as an untapped market with varying needs, preferences, and resources, instead of as unified block of helpless supplicants. Rather than treating them like criminals for not doing what we think they should, we should treat them like potential customers. If they don't like what is currently available, perhaps that is more of a commentary on the products than on the people who don't buy.

And in fact the uninsured are a varied lot – 59.9% of them are workers, 26.1% are not, and 13.9% are children. Of these workers, 21.1% are employed by very small firms (fewer than 10 employees), but another 21.1% work for companies with 1,000 or more employees: 29.2% are in service jobs, 21.6% are in sales or office work, but 17.6% work in "managerial or professional" capacities according to the EBRI report cited above.

Even more interesting is the family income level of the uninsured –

> 8.0 million earn under $10,000
> 7.7 million earn from $10,000 to $19,999
> 7.7 million earn from $20,000 to $29,999
> 6.1 million earn from $30,000 to $39,999
> 4.4 million earn from $40,000 to $49,999
> 6.7 million earn from $50,000 to $74,999
> 6.9 million earn over $75,000

As interesting as the demographic breakdowns are, the "psychographic" profile is even more enlightening. Three years after enactment of the law, CMS decided to finally ask the question: just who are these poor wretched uninsured people and what are they looking for? [98] One might think they would have inquired about this before enacting a remedy, but there you have it.

Turns out 92% of them can be divided into three segments:

1. The biggest cluster (47.8% of all the uninsured) are "healthy and young." They are not much motivated to enroll and they take their health for granted.
2. The next largest group (28.9%) are "sick, active and worried." These tend to be older and are pretty good candidates for coverage.
3. Finally we have the "passive and unengaged" group (15.3%). These folks tend to be older and have poor literacy skills.

These different people need different solutions.

The first group is unlikely to want to spend a lot of money on services they can't foresee needing. But they might like a Health Savings Account that allows them to be protected against catastrophe, while building up a sum of money for the future when they are more likely to need it.

The middle group would probably embrace comprehensive coverage if their expenses could be subsidized and they were assured of getting coverage.

The final group is made up of the people we wrote about above. They are not capable of understanding or navigating any health insurance system. They need the direct provision of care through neighborhood clinics and subsidized hospitals.

Unfortunately, the Affordable Care Act seems to be aimed solely at the middle group – the 29% of the uninsured who are sick and

---

[98] "Audience Segmentation for the Emerging Health Insurance Marketplace," CMS, https://marketplace.cms.gov/outreach-and-education/social-marketing-research-for-the-health-insurance-marketplace.pdf

worried. This is the stereotype rolled out by politicians who want to show off how much they care.

But their compassion seems to extend only to less than a third of the 16% of the population without insurance coverage – i.e. about five percent of the American population. So 95% of the country is being put through the wringer to benefit the 5% this law was written for.

Greg Scandlen

Conclusion

We have barely scratched the surface in this litany of failed policies. There is so much that could be added-

- The SCHIP (State Children's Health Insurance Program) that divorces children from their families in providing health insurance. The program did enroll children, but it would have worked even better to give the parents the money to add the kiddos to their own coverage as dependents. That way the whole family could have been in the same insurance plan instead of having to learn how separate plans work for different members of the family. [99]
- The idea of minimum "medical loss ratios," which make it almost impossible for companies to enter new markets or roll out new products. It also discourages anti-fraud measures. This had been tried in several states prior to Obamacare and failed every time. [100]
- The push for "evidence based medicine," which is a euphemism for "cookie cutter medicine." In fact, unlike health policy, medical practice has always been evidence based. That is why there are medical journals and continuing education programs for physicians. The new emphasis on "evidence based medicine" usually implies recognizing only those services that have been tested in a randomized, double blind clinical study, but, in fact, it would be unethical to subject much of what is done in medical care to such a process. Who would volunteer to be

---

[99] "State Children's Health Insurance Program (DCHP). Heartland Institute, May 2, 2007. https://www.heartland.org/publications-resources/publications/state-childrens-health-insurance-program-schip

[100] Greg Scandlen, "New Regulation Threatens Agents, HSA Plans," Health Policy Blog, NCPA, December 12, 2011. http://healthblog.ncpa.org/new-regulation-threatens-agents-hsa-plans/

part of the control group in testing the efficacy of setting broken bones? [101]

- The whole panoply of ideas that have been tried out and failed in demonstration projects – pay-for-performance, disease management, comparative effectiveness research, etc. [102] [103]

By the way, it isn't only in financing issues where the experts are wrong. For decades the nation has been whipsawed back and forth over dietary and behavioral commands that are later proven to be not only wrong, but with often disastrous effects --

- We were told to drink eight glasses of water every day, but it turns out we should drink water when we are thirsty.[104]
- We were told that eating animal fats would make us fat, but it turns out the real problem is sugar and carbohydrates. (This, after obesity and diabetes reach epidemic proportions.) [105] [106]
- We were told that second hand smoke was deadly, but it turns out it may be obnoxious but doesn't have many health consequences. (This, after smoking has been banned in virtually all workplaces and restaurants.) [107]

---

[101] Twila Brase, RN, PHN, "Evidence-Based Medicine: Rationing Care, Hurting Patients," The State Factor, ALEC, December 2008. http://www.cchfreedom.org/pdf/ebmstatefactorALECtwila.pdf

[102] John Goodman, PhD, "Why the Pilot Programs Failed" Health Policy Blog, NCPA, January 30, 2012, http://healthblog.ncpa.org/why-the-pilot-programs-failed/

[103] Arlene Weintrub, "Take Your Meds, Exercise, and Spend Billions," BusinessWeek, February 4, 2010. https://www.bloomberg.com/news/articles/2010-02-04/take-your-meds-exercise-and-spend-billions

[104] Honor Whiteman, "'Only Drink Water When Thirsty,' Study Suggests," Medical News Today, October 10, 2016. http://www.medicalnewstoday.com/articles/313389.php

[105] Kris Gunners, "Six Graphs That Show Why the 'War" on Fat was a Huge Mistake," Authority Nutrition. https://authoritynutrition.com/6-graphs-the-war-on-fat-was-a-mistake/

[106] Mark Hyman, MD, "Fat Does Not Make You Fat," http://drhyman.com/blog/2013/11/26/fat-make-fat/

All these decrees were proclaimed with absolute certainty from "the experts" on high. They are adopted by government agencies and imposed on a malleable population without a hint of doubt or uncertainty.

You may have noticed that we haven't dealt directly with ObamaCare -- the Affordable Care Act -- in this book. That is because ObamaCare didn't really break any new ground. Instead, it was a compilation of all of these already failed ideas. It took some 2,700 pages of legislative language but virtually every idea in this book can be found somewhere in the Affordable Care Act.

Which is pretty astonishing – down right pathological, if you think about it. I do not have a monopoly on the information presented here. It is widely available and widely known. The authors of ObamaCare could have found it if they wanted to. Yet somehow they thought it made sense to take dozens of failed ideas and put them all together in a single law. And then we were told we couldn't know what was in the bill until after it became law and was implemented.

What drives this kind of thinking?

Partly it is political. Political thinking is unlike anything you might encounter in business, engineering, medicine, or any other profession (except maybe law.) If you are used to staffing a political campaign or a Congressional office, you learn that your boss is never wrong – never – about anything. You cannot own up to any weakness. He or she must be presented as perfect in every way and so are his or her ideas. If they are criticized, your job is to attack the criticizer, not to examine the claims. Policy people, who may not be directly involved in politics, learn to do the same thing.

---

[107] Jacob Grier, "We Used Terrible Science to Justify Smoking Bans," Slate, February 13, 2017.
http://www.slate.com/articles/health_and_science/medical_examiner/2017/02/sec ondhand_smoke_isn_t_as_bad_as_we_thought.html

A policy proposal is defended against all criticism, no matter how valid. Political thinking poisons everything it touches.

Besides, you personally have nothing to lose by being wrong. You don't have to live with the consequences of your prescriptions. You haven't invested any of your own money in the project. Rockets won't explode on the launch pad. The new proposal will take years to implement and you will be out of Dodge by then. There is no cost to toying with other people's lives.

But it is also personal arrogance. There is a sense within "the Academy" that, having worked hard to earn a PhD, they are better than most people and don't have to answer to their lessors. They only have to please people who they see as their equals. This creates a sense of entitlement and "group think" bubble that can be deadly in public policy. We saw this during the Viet Nam War with Robert McNamara's "the best and the brightest" Defense Department management team, and more recently with the CIA's assessment of Iraq's "Weapons of Mass destruction."

The phenomenon of "the bubble" – that there is an educated elite that has little interaction with or affinity for the mass of Americans – has been written about quite a bit lately, with Charles Murray's "Belmont and Fishtown" [108] and Angelo Codevilla's "America's Ruling Class," [109] among others. But it is a natural outcome of Progressive ideology, which has dominated American intellectualism for the past 100 years. This is the belief that the masses of people are incapable of running their own affairs, so must be managed by a meritocracy of the educated elite.

Finally, there is a thread of Socialism, conscious or not, that contaminates much of the thinking among policy-makers. It shows up in the default position that government is good and the private

---

[108] Charles Murray, "Belmont & Fishtown," AEI, January 9, 2012. https://www.aei.org/publication/belmont-fishtown/
[109] Angelo Codevilla, "America's Ruling Class – And the Perils of Revolution," American Spectator, July 16, 2010. https://spectator.org/39326_americas-ruling-class-and-perils-revolution/

sector is not. Whatever the topic – veterans health services, prisons, the postal service, Social Security, K-12 education – any mention of performing the service better through the private sector is seen as heresy by many policy makers. It is really quite remarkable. There is little dispassionate consideration of the best way to get the job done and a whole lot of rhetoric about "the vagaries of the private market," as if the private sector is inherently evil and unfair, and only government can be trusted.

Taken together, these attitudes are so embedded there is little reason to hope for better results coming out of the public sector. Public policy will continue to lurch from failure to failure, never learning from mistakes, just repeating the same ones over and over.

Where does that leave us, as consumers of health care services? We have to learn to take control away from the bureaucrats. After all, every penny they spend on health care comes from us. There is no other source. It comes from us in the form of taxes, insurance premiums, or lost wages when our employers buy coverage for us. It is all our money. And it is supposed to be spent for our benefit.

We may have thought they would do a better job than we can in arranging how health care is delivered and paid for, but in fact they have done a horrible job. Everything they have tried has failed catastrophically. We don't need them. What we need is a doctor we trust who can work with us to get us the services we need.

We don't have to be experts in medical affairs any more than we have to be experts in tax law to file our taxes or in auto mechanics to get our car fixed. In any complex area we need the services of an agent – one who works for us and can be fired if they don't deliver. We can hire a physician to guide us through the complex maze of health care services. There are today many thousands of such doctors who are available to do exactly this. They are known as "concierge physicians." They will directly provide primary care services, but they will also act as our advocates in dealing with the rest of the health care system. Because we pay them directly, they can take the time to get to know us very well and know our preferences, our hopes and fears, and tailor services accordingly.

To make this work, we first need to get our money back. Get it back from the government agencies and insurance companies that currently control it. That means reducing our taxes and minimizing our insurance premiums. Fortunately, there is a vehicle to do exactly that – Health Savings Accounts (HSAs). The Republicans in Congress are currently working on making HSAs more flexible and widely available.

HSAs are primarily a way to get our money back. How you spend the money should be up to you. You may spend it to pay directly for services and bypass insurance company administrative costs. Or you might prefer to buy an insurance policy that will pay those bills for you. In turn, this could spawn a new generation of innovative insurance plans aimed at pleasing you – the consumer/buyer.

Either way, you are the customer, you control the money, and the insurance companies or providers of services want to make you happy so you will continue to patronize them. That is the only way we will ever succeed in making health care more affordable, more convenient, more accountable, far less bureaucratic, and of better quality. Just like everything else in America.

ABOUT THE AUTHOR

Greg Scandlen is an independent health care analyst in Waynesboro, Pennsylvania. He has nearly 40 years experience in health policy, especially in health care financing.

He started in the research department at Blue Cross Blue Shield of Maine in 1979, was recruited by the BCBS Association to go to Washington to work on state affairs in 1984.

Disturbed by the growth of managed care, he left the Blues in 1991 to organize the Council for Affordable Health Insurance where he helped get Medical Savings Accounts enacted. Once enacted, he went into independent consulting to help businesses adopt MSAs. He then did stints at the Cato Institute, the National Center for Policy Analysis, the Galen Institute, and finally organized Consumers for Health Care Choices in 2004, which is now a project of the Heartland Institute.

Throughout his career Mr. Scandlen has been an advocate of patient empowerment, consumer choice, and increased competition. He is a widely published author and blogger, has given hundreds of speeches throughout the country, and has been interviewed in many broadcast and print media outlets. His core insight is that most of the problems in the health care system stem from excessive reliance on third-party payment, and the solution lies in allowing health care consumers to control their own resources to purchase the services they value.